SAINT PETERSBURG

AND ITS SUBURBS

KT-871-392

History

ST PETERSBURG is a young city on a young river. Four thousand years ago, when the Egyptian pyramids had already been built, there was still no River Neva. From present-day Lake Ladoga to the modern shores of the Baltic the area was covered by a glacial sea. Then the land began to rise at a fairly rapid rate by geological standards. Ladoga became a lake that overflowed, pouring its waters across the watershed that now separated it from the sea. Some 2,500 years ago this mighty flow turned into a river that has still not properly settled into its banks – the number of islands in Neva's extensive delta is constantly changing.

Archaeological excavations at the mouth of the Okhta, a right-bank tributary of the Neva (actually older than its "parent" river!) uncovered an archaeological "layer cake", a sort of Troy on the Neva. It includes a 5000-year-old Neolithic site and the remains of three mediaeval fortresses: one Russian – Nevskoye Ustye and two Swedish – Landskrona and Nyenskans.

It is with Nyenskans that the history of St Petersburg begins. This stronghold stood on the border of Ingermanland, as the Swedes called the territory that they had taken from Russia in the early 17th century. Russia suffered deeply from its loss of access to the Baltic Sea and repeatedly tried to recover these old Novgorodian possessions. Only Peter the Great succeeded.

In the spring of 1703, his army moved down the Neva and, at the end of April, took Nyenskans. A council of war held on the night of 1 May decided not to reinforce the captured Swedish fortress, but instead to build a new strongpoint further down the Neva.

Going ashore on what would become the Petrograd Side on a day in May 1703, the Tsar was overcome by an inexpressible delight. He immediately fell in love with the place and without losing any time, the Tsar set about realizing his plan for the transformation of the Neva delta.

The scale and pace of the work were unprecedented. The city grew rapidly and within a decade it had acquired its own distinctive face, not customary for Russia. It was a European maritime city with straight streets, canals and landing-stages. The city was rationally and reliably protected: on the right bank the bastions of the Peter and Paul Fortress rose; on the left the fortified ramparts of the Admiralty, while beyond the

The Battle of Gangut on 27 July 1714. Engraved by Maurice Baquoi. 1724–27

Peter the Great. Detail of the painting *Peter I with an Allegorical Figure of Glory* by Jacopo Amigoni (Amiconi). Between 1732 and 1738

mouth of the Neva the naval fortress of Kronslot grew up literally from the water. South of the estuary suburban coastal residences sprang up and flourished – Peterhof, Yekaterinhof, Annenhof, Oranienbaum, Strelna, Dubki and, inland, Tsarskoye Selo.

In 1712 St Petersburg was proclaimed the capital of Russia. The court, institutions and officials moved here. The status of capital, and an imperial one at that (in 1721 Peter was proclaimed emperor), was a boon to St Petersburg, because for long decades after its founder's death, it was that function that kept the life in this city remote from the heart of Russia.

St Petersburg had a "Dutch childhood". If you take a look at the young city "in profile" – by viewing the urban landscape in the engravings of Alexei Zubov, then you might confidently call it "Dutch". We see tall attractive buildings tightly pressed against one another along the embankments as in Amsterdam, typically Dutch spires – spikes with pennants and flags flying from them, as one can still find in Holland today. In the engravings it is also possible to spot that the drawbridges were also made with Dutch-style counterweights resembling bending storks, and they are painted with whitewash as is still done even now in the Netherlands. Add to that a host of typically Dutch windmills on the spit of Vasilyevsky Island, on the Okhta, and even on the bastions of the Peter and Paul Fortress.

When he sent the architect Ivan Korobov to study abroad in 1724, Peter ordered him to go straight to Holland: "You need to live in Holland and study the manner of Dutch architecture, and especially the foundations that I need here: just as low-lying, just as much water; the same thin walls are needed… How to lay out their gardens, decorate them with groves of trees and also the sorts of figures that nowhere in the world do they do so well as in Holland." He also said: "God grant me health and St Petersburg will be a second Amsterdam!" Later, when the capital expanded and was reconstructed under the influence of other styles, "Dutch Petersburg" drowned, as it were, dissolved, disappeared into the foundations and was lost behind the facades of the new buildings. But to remind us of its "Dutch childhood" we have the spires of the SS Peter and Paul Cathedral and the Admiralty, which have retained the shapes given to them when the Dutchman Harmann van Boles raised them, and also the chimes that were made to sound by the Dutch craftsman Oort Krass.

Menshikov's estate and the ambassadorial palace on Vasilyevsky Island in St Petersburg. Engraved by Alexei Zubov. 1715

Peter I.
Artist: Valentin Serov. 1907

THE REIGN of Peter's daughter Elizabeth (1741–1761) saw the Baroque in its most vivid, fanciful and spectacular "Italian manner". The man who became the Empress's chief architect was Francesco Bartolomeo Rastrelli, one of the most fortunate exponents of that profession in the world, who managed to translate the majority of his projects into bricks and mortar, to realize a whole host of ideas – and all thanks to his generous crowned employer. Elizabeth was a true daughter of the Baroque, fond of luxury in clothing, in the interior décor and external appearance of buildings, and she never begrudged money for that purpose. The Empress's chief architect was Francesco Bartolomeo Rastrelli, one of the most fortunate exponents of that profession in the world, who managed to translate the majority of his projects into bricks and mortar, to realize a whole host of ideas – and all thanks to his generous crowned employer.

Posterity not without reason considers Rastrelli's unsurpassed merit to lie in the sheer scope of his architectural concepts in combination with a sense of proportion, harmony, symmetry that avoids tedium, precise layouts, concision and refinement of forms. It is as if his edifices (the Winter Palace in St Petersburg, the Catherine Palace at Tsarskoye Selo, the Great Peterhof Palace and many others) are still inhabited by his jovial genius that smiles upon us each time we look at these incomparable creations in turquoise and azure. Astonishingly these buildings created by an Italian "in the Italian taste" turned out Russian in spirit. Nowhere else in the world at that time were structures in the Baroque style erected on such a gigantic scale as in Russia. At the same time they display features of a recognizably Russian, Muscovite architectural tradition, while also being Europeanly elegant and light-hearted. They tell us that human beings were made not for suffering, but for happiness and the enjoyment of life.

UNDER Catherine II (1762–1796) a very different architectural style almost instantly became dominant: the fanciful Baroque gave way to austere, majestic Neo-Classicism. This matched the Empress's tastes and accorded with the outlook of the Enlightenment – the chief tendency in intellectual life at that time. That is not to say there was a campaign to demolish or reconstruct the works of Elizabethan Baroque. It was a distinctive feature of this era that the architects were capable of preserving what had been

Panorama of the Neva with a view of the Peter and Paul Fortress. Engraved by Yefim Vinogradov after a drawing by Mikhail Makhayev. 1753

Empress Elizabeth. Artist: Heinrich Buchholtz. Last quarter of the 18th century

created before them and to combine new architecture with old. Neo-Classicism itself underwent a certain evolution in Russia. At first it was strongly influenced by the ideas of French Neo-Classicism. That was the style in which Jean-Baptiste Vallin de La Mothe worked and he became effectively the leading architect of the first half of Catherine II's reign. Then, roughly in the 1780s, the elevated and somewhat austere architecture of the French school was superseded by the clear, exquisite forms of Italian Neo-Classicism. Particularly popular were the many buildings designed by Giacomo Quarenghi, whose chief rival was British-born Charles Cameron. The most important monument from Catherine's time (indeed, in the whole history of the city) must be reckoned to be the celebrated *Bronze Horseman* by the French sculptor Falconet, which became immediately and for all time a symbol of imperial St Petersburg.

Catherine's Neo-Classicism to a large extent shaped the present-day appearance of the city. Thanks to its astonishing qualities rooted in Antiquity, a majestic orderliness took firm hold of St Petersburg. In Catherine's time the suburban-type housing areas quickly began to disappear, while the vacant lots and marshland separating different parts of the city were built on. The principle of architectural ensembles became a feature of urban development – whole complexes of buildings united not so much by the earlier idea of "regularity" as by the concept of harmony.

ALEXANDER I'S era (1801–1825) completed the formation of St Petersburg's appearance as "the façade of the empire", its grand display case. For the first time the city presented to the eye in full measure that exceptional harmony of buildings, sky and water that still enchants people today. The austere Classicism of Catherine's time "swallowed" Paul I's gloomy castle and fused with Alexander's sumptuous Empire to form, together with the glittering pearls of the past age of the Baroque, St Petersburg's famous architectural symphony. Andrei Voronikhin, Andreyan Zakharov and Carlo Rossi were its chief composers under Alexander I. "One has to part with Petersburg," the poet Batiushkov wrote in 1811, "… for a time, to see ancient capitals – decrepit Paris, sooty London – to appreciate the value of Petersburg. Look – what unity! How all the parts correspond to the whole! What beauty in the buildings, what taste and on the whole

Catherine II as Legislatrix in the Temple of Justice. Artist: Dmitry Levitsky. Early 1780s

View of the Exchange and Admiralty from the Peter and Paul Fortress. Artist: Feodor Alexeyev. 1810

Alexander I. Artist: George Dawe. 1826

what variety that comes from the mixing of water with buildings. Look at the railing of the Summer Garden that is reflected in the greenery of the limes, elms and oaks! What lightness and proportion there is in its design!"

NICHOLAS I'S St Petersburg (1825–1855) was quite different from Alexander I's, which had resembled an enormous building site with a maze of fences enclosing the edifices under construction. Now, in Nicholas's time, those works were not merely completed, but resplendent in their enduring beauty. The brilliant Carlo Rossi completed the triumphal ensemble of the General Staff building and never again built anything or even took up a pencil. But he left us the ensemble of the Alexandrinsky Theatre and the buildings of the Senate and Synod, linked by an arch and resembling a church organ with their dozens of columns. Nicholas's reign saw the blossoming of the talent of Auguste Ricard de Montferrand, who devoted all his efforts to the erection of St Isaac's Cathedral. The Frenchman was a remarkable engineer. When the Tsar and his whole family came to watch the installation of the first column for the cathedral on 20 March 1828 they did not have to wait long – the raising of the immense stone cylinder took just 45 minutes. But Montferrand's greatest feat of engineering was raising in 100 minutes the Alexander Column in the centre of Palace Square.

And yet sumptuous Empire-style St Petersburg also became a thing of the past. Tastes gradually changed, new requirements arose. The bustle of the European industrial revolution reached the Russian capital. New materials and new techniques appeared. Architects began to find the rigorous bounds of the Empire style constricting; the era of a free choice of styles had arrived. Montferrand stubbornly completed St Isaac's Cathedral which had become old-fashioned for the time, but he was already thinking of another style, seeking inspiration in Renaissance works. Nicholas I himself also felt drawn to new forms, becoming a devotee of the Neo-Gothic. As if in secret, hidden from his grand Empire-style capital, he constructed for himself, for personal pleasure, a special "Gothic" world in his beloved Peterhof. The Neo-Gothic suited the cast of Nicholas's mind – the role of the noble crusader knight, defending the "old order" and the Orthodox religion, was one that appealed to him. He wanted to live not

The Formal Inauguration of the Alexander Column on Palace Square in St Petersburg on 30 August 1834. Artist: Adolphe Ladurner. 1834

Nicholas I. Artist: Yegor Botman. 1856

in the gilded interior of a palace on view from all sides, but on his "country estate", in a small cosy house, built, like in England, close to the ruins of the family's ancestral castle and close to an old chapel that had sunk into the ground and whose stone floor was worn down by the shoes of dozens of generations of parishioners. That was his "Cottage", his favourite suburban residence. New times were coming.

WHILE Nicholas I, as one of the younger sons in the imperial family, had not been prepared for the throne in childhood and adolescence, his own son and heir, Alexander II, received from an early age a thorough preparation for the burden of rulership. He was educated and intelligent and although he lacked the decisiveness of his younger brother, Konstantin, he grasped the pressing need for reforms in the country and was inwardly ready for them. The reforms were a long time maturing in heated debates; gradually too society was "warmed" to accept such initially off-puttingly radical changes as the abolition of serfdom, the introduction of rural self-government, trial by jury and reform of the army. Alexander was consistent in his movement towards a new political system for the country that he envisaged with a parliament and the basic civil liberties. The Tsar also undoubtedly possessed great personal courage not to be intimidated by the attempts made on his life by terrorists who hoped by assassinating the autocrat to unleash a revolution in the country and so organized an out-and-out hunt for Alexander II – trying seven times to kill him. The bomb thrown by a terrorist alongside the Catherine Canal on 1 March 1881 put an end to his great life and to his great reforms.

Alexander II's reforms transformed the country. A boom in industrial and railway construction followed. The era of capitalism dawned with all its merits and shortcomings. Architecture also changed. New social demands, in which economics played an ever-growing part, new building techniques and materials, progressive artistic ideas in conjunction with the freedoms and competition inevitable under capitalism smashed the monopoly of a single style. In architecture, as in life more generally, an artistic free-for-all began. The abandoning of adherence to the principles of any one style and the combination in a single project of elements and devices of various styles taken from a broad

Panorama of
St Petersburg
from the Belfry
of the SS Peter
and Paul Fortress.
Lithograph by
Charles Claude
Bachelier after
a drawing by
Giuseppe Raimondo
Bernardazzi.
1850s

Alexander II.
Artist: Yegor
Botman. 1875

architectural heritage, led to the emergence of the eclectic tendency. There were also various "revivals", reproducing one or another single historical style, such as the Gothic or Renaissance. Such masterpieces as St Basil's in Moscow inspired the Pseudo-Russian style of the Saviour on the Spilt Blood; a fascination with the Orient brought the Moresque style to St Petersburg in, for example, the Muruzi House, while a love of Rastrelli and his fellow geniuses gave birth to the Neo-Baroque. Eclecticism and the revivals proved very important for St Petersburg. They shaped the appearance of the historic part of the city as a whole. A tremendous role in this process was played by the taste of the customer and the contractor. Eclecticism produced both crude banalities and high art. The brilliant architect Andrei Stakenschneider was an unsurpassed exponent of retrospective styles already in Nicholas I's time, giving preference to the Neo-Renaissance and Neo-Baroque. Somewhat later Nikolai Benois also became famed.

ALEXANDER III (1881–1894), who came to power after the terrorists killed his father, was a man with a different mentality. He was convinced that the westernizing course chosen by his father during the Great Reforms did not accord with Russia's true interests. Prompted by his mentor, the conservative Konstantin Pobedonostsev, he advanced the idea that Russia had its own path, that it did not need a parliament, that its lifeblood was the closeness between the autocracy and the deeply religious common people. Consequently he abandoned his father's reforms and put Russia "into the deep freeze", seeking to preserve the regime of "popular autocracy" – an illusion for which his son, Nicholas II, would later pay dearly.

Towards the end of the imperial period a new style began to emerge from eclecticism, glistening with glass and steel (like the celebrated globe on the Singer Company building that is now the House of Books). This was the Moderne, the Russian variant of the Art Nouveau. With new materials and new ideas it was possible to disregard the old canons, to build with a free inventiveness. Asymmetrical layouts, complex sculpted facades, windows and bays of various shapes, elegant decorative details – all this made Moderne-era buildings picturesque, entertaining and convenient to use. St Petersburg became home to the "Northern Moderne" which gave preference to

Alexander III.
Artist: Ivan
Tiurin. 1890

Landing-Stage
on the Neva.
Artist: Alexander
Beggrow. 1885

modest colours, local materials and the northerners' general spirit of restraint. Notable among its exponents was the architect Feodor Lidval. But the Moderne was a style for the rich and they were keen to put their wealth on display, disregarding their more humble neighbours and nearby masterpieces from the past. One such "money-bags" that elbowed its way in was the shop created on Nevsky Prospekt for the Yeliseyev merchant family by the architect Gavriil Baranovsky. But, after enduring along with the city all the terrible trials of the 20th century, Yeliseyev's has long since become our own, familiar, Petersburg money-bags, impoverished like all the rest.

MANY considered Nicholas II (1894–1917) a deceitful person, secretive and indifferent to others. He did not have the mind to make an outstanding politician and seemed to be a mediocrity in all things. His reign can be divided into two parts: before and after the abortive 1905 revolution. In the first period Nicholas, opposed to any sort of liberalism, tried to avoid the political reforms that were overdue, trusting in the strength of the autocratic tradition. In the second he grudgingly conceded them. It was the mismatch between his archaic views and the real political situation in the country that led Nicholas, and Russia with him, to catastrophe in 1917. By the end of his reign the Tsar had lost the support of all strata of society and his overthrow was welcomed by the majority of Russia's people. Russia's unfortunate experience in the First World War prepared the ground for insurrection. After being deposed in February 1917, Nicholas II was savagely killed together with his wife and children at Yekaterinburg in the summer of 1918.

Nevsky Prospekt
and the square
by Gostiny Dvor
in 1900

Nicholas II.
Artist: Ilya Repin.
1896

IT SO HAPPENS that all three Russian revolutions began in St Petersburg (renamed Petrograd in 1914). While the first revolution that began in 1905 with the shooting down of a peaceful demonstration of workers approaching Palace Square led to the establishment of constitutional order, the formation of political parties and the State Duma (parliament), the second, in February 1917, ended with the overthrow of autocracy and the proclamation of a republic. But the Provisional (pending a constituent assembly) Government formed from the parliamentary parties failed to hold on

to power and in October 1917 it was deposed by the Bolsheviks and other left-wing semi-underground parties drawing on the support of the soviets (councils of workers and soldiers), Their irresponsible propaganda was aimed at society's lowest, who longed for "social justice", which they understood as the confiscation of property, the elimination of "hostile classes" with the goal of constructing a "classless society". After forming a Soviet government the Bolsheviks, led by Lenin and Trotsky, dispersed the Constituent Assembly and shot down a demonstration in support of it. Then the Bolsheviks proclaimed their "Red Terror" and unleashed a bloody civil war. After removing the front that was holding back the Kaiser's forces, the Soviet government feared that the Germans would take the capital and in the early hours of 3 March 1918 it fled from Petrograd to Moscow. From that moment Petrograd ceased to be the capital, although it remained an important centre for the country. In 1924, after the death of Lenin, the city was renamed Leningrad.

THE SIEGE OF LENINGRAD

FOR LENINGRAD, like the rest of the Soviet Union, the Second World War began on 22 June 1941. By early September the invading Germans were at the gates of the city. Quite quickly, with the aid of the Finns who came from the north, the Führer's forces closed the circle around Leningrad.

Hitler decided not to storm the city, but to starve it into submission and reduce it to rubble with constant air-raids and artillery bombardments. With pedantry coupled with cold cruelty, day after day large-calibre shells were fired into Leningrad, high-explosive and incendiary bombs dropped from the sky. Soon the snow-bound city was without electricity, heating and running water and starvation began. The daily ration issued to non-workers in the winter of 1941/42 amounted to just 125 grammes (less than 4½ ounces) of bread. People died right on the streets; corpses lay in the apartments and stairwells. It is believed that Leningrad lost at least a million and a half people during the siege, with 97% being due to starvation. People reacted in various ways to those monstrous, inhuman conditions, but the overwhelming majority of Leningraders dis-

The cruiser Aurora, a symbol of the October Revolution of 1917

The *Motherland* statue at Piskarevskoye Memorial Cemetery

played their best qualities. It was such people with their unparalleled steadfastness, who, together with the troops on the Leningrad and Karelian fronts and the volunteer militia – ordinary citizens freezing and starving in the trenches around Leningrad, saved the honour of Peter's city and did not permit the German army to parade down Nevsky Prospekt. The siege was broken in January 1943, but finally lifted only a year later. The long rows of gigantic common graves at Piskarevskoye Memorial Cemetery and other places in the city are now a precious shrine and will remain forever a place of veneration and prayer for Petersburgers.

THE CITY ABOVE THE FREE NEVA

THE TERRIBLE wounds inflicted on the city during the 900-day siege took years to heal.

The break-up of the Soviet Union in 1991 again changed life in the city. It recovered its original birth name – "Saint Petersburg". Churches reopened; the restoration of many abandoned and decrepit historical buildings began; new museums opened; one after another monuments appeared honouring people who had brought fame to St Petersburg. In 1998, the remains of Nicholas II and members of his family shot in Yekaterinburg in 1918 were laid to rest in the SS Peter and Paul Cathedral, the burial place of the Russian emperors. In 2003 the city celebrated its 300th anniversary with great pomp in a series of events. Specially for the occasion the Konstantinovsky Palace at Strelna that was almost ruined beyond repair was restored and reconstructed to become "the Maritime Residence of the President of the Russian Federation", the start of the realization of a plan to transfer some federal institutions from Moscow to St Petersburg. The first to make the move was the Constitutional Court, which is now housed in the building of the Senate. New technology made it possible to light the architectural monuments in the city centre in a striking way, while the bridges over the Neva were embellished with coloured garlands.

Celebrating
the city's
birthday on
Nevsky Prospekt

CLOSE to the right bank of the Neva, on a small sandy island overgrown with shrubs, on 16 May 1703 a fortress was founded and called after St Peter – Sankt-Piter-Burkh. Later the name of the citadel (in a more German form) was extended to the city that began to grow alongside it.

The fortress was built to a plan drawn up by foreign engineers with the participation of Peter I. In 1706 the Swiss architect Domenico Trezzini began to reconstruct the earthwork bastions in masonry.

The heart of the fortress is the SS Peter and Paul Cathedral, begun in 1712 on the site of the first, wooden church. It, too, was designed by Domenico Trezzini. In Peter's lifetime only the bell-tower was constructed, with a spire topped by a ball, a cross and a weathervane in the form of a flying angel. The figure was created by the Dutch craftsman Herman van Boles.

This slender, yet powerful shaft resembles the main mast of Peter's ship-like fortress. Its gilded spire, soaring to a height of 122 metres, is the first to catch the golden ray of the rising sun and then it shines on throughout the day, delighting the eyes and hearts of Petersburgers. The reflection of the spire – a fascinating track of gold – extends across the grey waves of the Neva from the fortress almost to the opposite left bank. Perhaps the angel uses it now and again to come down and rest from its onerous duties – blessing and protecting this sinful city. From Peter's time onwards the cathedral served as the burial place of the rulers of Russia.

The fortress's 300 guns were intended to reliably protect the city, but the citadel was never tested – the mighty fortifications of Kronstadt and a strong navy made it impossible for a foe to even enter the Neva. And the fortress turned into a "Russian Bastille". Its bastions and ravelins were converted into prisons that were as terrible as any in Russia.

The main, Petrovsky or St Peter's Gate of the fortress is the oldest. This is more than just the way in. It is a triumphal arch topped by a double-headed eagle for victors to enter through.

Passing that gate and the next, you come to the St John Bridge that takes you off the island. Below the bridge you can see atop a free-standing pile a metal hare in a cowering pose, which every child that goes over the bridge wants to save from the spreading river.

The Boat House

Sculpture
of Peter I

The Peter and Paul
Fortress

The angel atop
the spire of the
SS Peter and Paul
Cathedral

A putto on the
roof of the belfry

A view of
the fortress
from Palace
Embankment

The SS Peter and
Paul Cathedral

The nave of the
SS Peter and Paul
Cathedral with
a view of the
iconostasis

The Tsar's Place
and the pulpit

The tomb of
Emperor Peter I

The memorial
above the burial
place of Emperor
Nicholas II and his
family

St John's
(Ioannovsky) Bridge

The Naryshkin
Bastion

St Peter's Gate

Detail of the relief
*Simon the Magus
Cast Down by the
Apostle Peter* and
the heraldic eagle
above the arch of
St Peter's Gate

The statue of *Valour*
in a niche by
St Peter's Gate

Palace Square

WHICHEVER way you approach Palace Square, a splendid view opens out before you. But when you walk along Bolshaya Morskaya Street and pass through the gigantic arch of the General Staff to find yourself faced with the Winter Palace, it is as if a curtain is suddenly raised to reveal one of the magnificent architectural landscapes on the planet. People are struck dumb and motionless by the sudden splendour of the immense square with the Alexander Column in the middle, the striking Baroque backdrop of the Winter Palace with its flickering windows and the Admiralty spire shining off to the left.

The square acquired its present form after 1819 when the architect Carlo Rossi began to construct his unique edifice for the department of war. The greatness of the architect's special talent lay in the ability not simply to construct one or two attractive buildings next to each other, but to produce an integrated ensemble that combined solemn Empire grandeur with pure, clear architectural ideas, refined and balanced proportions – in short, with "precise beauty". Rossi displayed a subtle sense for the spirit of the imperial capital when he proposed to unite the buildings lining Palace Square behind the majestic curve of the General Staff (1823–29). I Then he cut in the middle of that curve not simply a passage through to Nevsky Prospekt, but a huge 28-metre-high archway, turning it into a grand triumphal arch adorned by a chariot driven by the goddess of victory and military trophies, celebrating Russia's achievements in defeating Napoleon.

Petersburgers are convinced that the Alexander Column is the most beautiful in the world: mighty, yet elegant, well-proportioned and restrained. On top of everything, this granite monolith 25 metres tall stands alone on a bed of piles without any additional support. It was created and raised in 1832 by Auguste Ricard de Montferrand, the architect of St Isaac's Cathedral. The column is devoted to Emperor Alexander I, the vanquisher of Napoleon, and the angel at the top of the column has Alexander's face.

Besides the General Staff, Palace Square is formed by the Staff of the Corps of Guards and the complex of the Hermitage, one of the world's greatest museums.

A double-headed eagle on the entrance gate of the Winter Palace

The Chariot of Glory above the Arch of the General Staff

Palace Square with a view of the Winter Palace and the Alexander Column

The General
Staff building

The Arch of
the General
Staff seen
from Bolshaya
Morskaya Street

The angel on
the top of the
Alexander
Column

The State Hermitage

THE MUSEUM is housed in a complex of five large buildings constructed at various times. The chief element of the complex is Francesco Bartolomeo Rastrelli's masterpiece, the Winter Palace that served as the imperial residence, besides which there are the Hermitage Theatre and the museum buildings that were constructed alongside as the Russian monarchs' collections of art grew: the Small Hermitage, Large (or Old) Hermitage and New Hermitage. In addition the Hermitage now possesses a considerable section of the General Staff building.

The Winter Palace, built by Rastrelli in 1756–62 for Peter's daughter, Elizabeth, became an embodiment of the might of the Russian monarchy. Rastrelli was known for building quickly, but the great architect was never willing to compromise proper practice for speed. He insisted that each day one row of bricks could be laid around the entire perimeter of the building, so the "each brick that goes into the work will bind with the mortar in air for twenty-four hours, [otherwise] dryness and strength will not come for many years." It was probably in this considered lack of haste that the secret of the old master-builders lay – after all, their creations have not been destroyed by time, or shells, or the onslaughts of the ignorant and they still stand to this day, amazing us, who have grown used to the sight of crumbling concrete and silicate bricks, with their unassailable, truly enduring strength "for the sole glory of the Russian Empire" (as a 1757 decree put it).

The dimensions and splendour of the palace, both inside and out, astonished contemporaries. The rulers' formal entrances, receptions and balls took place in the state rooms that were located in the main, second storey of the Winter Palace, reached by the splendid Jordan Staircase, which got its name from the custom of cutting a hole in the ice of the river, known as a Jordan, for the Orthodox ritual of Blessing the Waters at Epiphany (6 January) each year.

The Winter Palace might be likened to a huge liner sailing through time. Besides the grand public state rooms and living quarters (the private apartments), it contained two churches, a theatre, a museum, gardens, a telegraph station, a pharmacy with a laboratory, offices, numerous kitchens, storerooms, cellars, laundries, stables, a riding school, carriage houses and accommodation for the staff. There were 4,000 servants

A Scythian gold comb

Diamond badge based on the monogram of Catherine II

who lived permanently in the palace. It also had its own army – palace grenadiers and sentries from the guards regiments. In the 1920s and '30s the Winter Palace underwent a tremendous reconstruction: 1,150 rooms with various purposes were converted into halls for the display of painting, sculpture and other works of art. Today the museum's displays are spread over more than 350 halls.

The Hermitage as a museum began with Catherine II who decided to transfer the art treasures that she kept in secret rooms in the Winter Palace to a new home in a pavilion constructed by Yury Veldten and Jean-Baptiste Vallin de La Mothe that became known as the "hermitage", meaning "a place of solitude".

The imperial art collection gradually grew; its sumptuous home was enlarged in the 1780s with the building of the Large Hermitage (architect: Yury Veldten) t, and then, in the middle of the 19th century, the museum complex was completed by the New Hermitage (architect: Leo von Klenze) with its celebrated portico on Millionnaya Street. The roof of the portico is supported on the shoulders of ten atlantes. These figures were created from Serdobol granite by the sculptor Alexander Terebenev from a sketch by von Klenze, A walkway from the Large (Old) Hermitage leads to the building of the Hermitage Theatre, built by Giacomo Quarenghi in 1787 on the bank of the picturesque little Winter Canal that evokes a host of literary associations.

Today the most precious of all the Hermitage's treasures (which number almost 15,000 paintings, 12,000 sculptures, 600,000 works of graphic art, just as many archaeological finds, and much more) is the gallery of Western European painting and sculpture. There are pictures by Leonardo da Vinci, Raphael, Velazquez, El Greco, Rembrandt, Rubens, Titian, Van Dyck, Poussin, Watteau and Chardin, and also works by outstanding sculptors from Michelangelo to Canova, Falconet, Houdon and others. The top floor of the Hermitage is the realm of the Impressionists. On display there are paintings by Renoir, Monet, Cézanne, Van Gogh, Gauguin, Matisse and Picasso, as well as sculpture by Rodin.

One could literally spend weeks going from hall to hall in the Hermitage and enjoying masterpieces from all periods and parts of the world.

Leonardo da Vinci. *The Litta Madonna*

Henri Matisse. *The Red Room*

A view of the
Winter Palace
and Palace
Embankment
from Palace
Bridge

The portico of the
New Hermitage

A double-headed
eagle on the
entrance gate of
the Winter Palace

The Small Throne
Room (Peter the
Great Hall)

The Main
(Jordan) Staircase

The Armorial Hall

The Gallery
of 1812

The Peacock Clock
in the Pavilion
Hall

The Pavilion Hall

The Large Skylight
Hall

A view of the
Rembrandt Room
from the Council
Staircase

The Hall of
Flemish Painting

The Jupiter Hall

The display of
sculpture in the
Gallery of the
History of Ancient
Painting

The Raphael
Loggias

St Isaac's Cathedral

ST ISAAC'S Cathedral, which looms majestically, like a patriarch, above the city, was the life's work of French architect and engineer Auguste Ricard de Montferrand, who arrived in Russia in 1816 and worked in St Petersburg right up to his death in 1858.

The cathedral had a long history before Montferrand. A wooden church, consecrated to the obscure Orthodox saint Isaac of Dalmatia, on whose day Peter I had been born, was put up in 1710, but two attempts by later architects to build a masonry cathedral on the site ended in failure and their works had to be dismantled due to the instability of the marshy soil beneath them. As a matter of fact, Montferrand began building his church in 1818 on the site of Antonio Rinaldi's unfinished effort and the Frenchman used the foundations of that building and part of its walls.

St Isaac's Cathedral rests on a raft of piles, tar-impregnated logs 6½ metres long. Above the piles Montferrand constructed a massive continuous foundation of granite slabs and rubble. Another original idea was to raise the granite columns (all 112 of them!) before the walls of the cathedral were constructed. Raising each column was accomplished in a matter of minutes thanks to Montferrand's inventiveness. The whole city, including the imperial family, would gather to watch the huge cylinders of stone being set in place.

The outside and especially the inside decoration of the cathedral was astonishingly luxurious. Only a state as powerful and wealthy as the Russian Empire could afford to decorate its chief place of worship with so much marble and expensive semiprecious stones. The deep rich tone of St Isaac's dome was achieved by laborious efforts; the copper sheets covering it were coated with a gold amalgam and then the mercury was evaporated off. This was repeated three times. The columns of the iconostasis were faced with Urals malachite and Badakhshan lapis-lazuli. The cathedral was painted and decorated with mosaics by the foremost artists of the time, led by Karl Briullov, while the sculptures were made by the leaders in that branch of art: Nikolai Pimenov, Ivan Vitali and others.

Part of the dome
of St Isaac's Cathedral

The stained-glass
window of *The
Resurrection* behind
the altar

St Isaac's Cathedral

The iconostasis of St Isaac's Cathedral

The vaults of St Isaac's Cathedral

Angels with a lamp on the roof of St Isaac's Cathedral

St Isaac's Square

GOLD-DOMED St Isaac's that gave its name to the square did not make it a mere open space in front of its majestic portal; it did not suppress the square, but rather set it free to join the bustling life of the city. In contrast to the neighbouring squares, St Isaac's and the square in front of the Mariinsky Palace, with which it merges, seem to be a huge junction of the near-dozen streets and lanes that run into them. Here there is an endless flow of traffic and hurrying pedestrians and the square seems to dissolve in the body of the living city. It is not surprising that as far back as the start of the 20th century, St Isaac's, along with those by the railway station, had the most commercial appearance among St Petersburg's squares and bore some resemblance to places in the business districts of Vienna, Berlin or Budapest.

This impression is to a large extent due to the utterly Europeanized appearance of the Astoria, one of the city's best hotels. It was built by Feodor Lidval in 1912. Occupying a prominent corner between Bolshaya Morskaya Street and St Isaac's Square, the hotel immediately began to play a dominant role in this part of the city. Yet the Astoria did not spoil the architectural environment of the square that consisted of Neo-Classical buildings from the 18th and 19th centuries: the Miatlevs' house, buildings belonging to the Ministry of State Properties and the Lobanov-Rostovsky Palace. Nor did its height belittle the monument to Emperor Nicholas I unveiled in 1859. It has a very unusual feature that has won it a place in art history. The figure of the horse (and its rider) was created for the monument designed by Montferrand by Piotr Klodt, Russia's best sculptor of horses. He "raised" the mighty bronze steed in a canter, and froze it for a moment on just its two hind legs. It seems that in an instant it will lower its front hooves, obedient to the will of the imperious horseman. Everything else in this sculptural group (the symbolic female figures, the bas-reliefs and the rest) seems secondary and even unimportant, so strongly do the magnificent prancing steed and the rider firmly in the saddle captivate the viewer. Those that disliked a monarch, who was not the most talented or successful, used the appearance of his equestrian statue dashing in the same direction as the *Bronze Horseman* as the occasion for a joke: no matter how Emperor Nicholas galloped he would never manage to catch up with Peter the Great. But in terms of skill as a sculptor, Klodt certainly "caught up" with Falconet.

The Mariinsky Palace

The Monument to Nicholas I

Senate Square

FOR TWO centuries this square open to all the winds off the Neva (Decembrists' Square from 1923 to 2008) was the location of the highest judicial and ecclesiastical authorities for the huge country. It also retains the memory of the events of 14 December 1825. On that day rebellious officers, later called Decembrists, brought their soldiers onto the square, but forces loyal to the government fired grapeshot into the ranks of mutineers.

On the square stands an equestrian monument to Peter the Great. This is the city's most famous monument, the symbol of St Petersburg. It was the creation of the Frenchman Etienne Maurice Falconet, who worked on the project from 1768. The sculptor immediately revealed to Catherine II, who had invited him to Russia, how he envisaged the monument to Peter: "I shall confine myself to just a statue of this hero, whom I shall treat neither as a great general nor as a victor, although he was, of course, both those things. Far higher is the personality of the creator, the legislator, the benefactor of his country, and that is what needs to be shown to people. My Tsar does not hold any baton; he extends his beneficent right hand over the country he is travelling. He is ascending a rock that serves him as a pedestal – that is an emblem of the difficulties he overcame." The inscription on the pedestal was revised by Catherine personally and states laconically: "TO PETER THE FIRST / CATHERINE THE SECOND 1782" – in Russian on one side, in Latin on the other. And ever since then the Bronze Horseman, as the statue came to be known in the 19th century following the publication of Pushkin's poem of that name, has been amazing the public with its exceptional power, some sort of magical force that it seems to exude.

In the late 1820s Senate Square acquired the appearance we know today, when the celebrated architect Carlo Rossi reconstructed the old Senate building. Again, as with the building for the General Staff, Rossi managed not just to construct two majestic edifices next to each other – for the Governing Senate and Most Holy Synod – but to create an architectural ensemble. To achieve this he spanned Galernaya Street that separates the two buildings with an elegant arch. Todaythe Senate is home to the Constitutional Court, while the Synod contains the Boris Yeltsin Presidential Library.

The sculpture of Peter the Great as *Carpenter Tsar* on Admiralty Embankment

Senate Square

The *Bronze Horseman* monument to Peter the Great

The Admiralty

THE "starting point" of the city's main thoroughfare, Nevsky Prospekt, is the building of the Admiralty with a golden ship atop its spire. This version was built in 1806–11 by the architect Andreyan Zakharov on the site of Peter I's Admiralty, where Russia's first naval ships were built and launched. It is simply unfathomable how this man managed to create a masterpiece of incomparable grandeur and exquisite harmony from an ordinary industrial-barrack-and-storage facility almost half a kilometre in length; how he managed to give it a new, grand, festive look, to make the building's extensive façade powerful, yet unwearying and attractive. And the magic of the Admiralty tower, which has become another symbol of St Petersburg, speaks for itself – it is so well-proportioned and elegant that it never even occurs to us that we are looking at a huge monumental structure. Moreover Zakharov the magician gave this construction not just harmony but also some mysterious power that for two centuries already has been drawing eyes away from the mundane scurry and noise of Nevsky Prospekt or the other two central streets that disperse ray-like from the Admiralty, and up the faces of the golden spire to the little ship to heaven, to eternity, to God…

Beneath the walls of the Admiralty are the rustling maples and limes of the Alexander Garden. It was created in 1874 on much of what was once the glacis – an open area around the fortified shipyard that protected against both enemies and fire. This later became Admiralty Square, connecting Palace Square with Senate Square to produce a gigantic parade ground on which almost the whole Russian army would form up and march, while in winter it served as a setting for popular festivities. The garden, named after Emperor Alexander II, was intended for the common people, who travelled here from the outskirts to stroll its lengthy alleys and view the monuments to leading writers and scientists dotted around the park. Now it provides a charming shady refuge in which to rest after a long walk up busy Nevsky. Protected by the mighty body of the Admiralty from the Neva's merciless winds, the garden is particularly pleasant in autumn, when yellow and red leaves slowly tumble from the maples, and children's voices carry from the playground…

The ship weathervane on the Admiralty spire

Trumpeting spirits of Glory above the arch throught the Admiralty tower

The tower of the Admiralty

Nevsky Prospekt

NEVSKY is an unusual street, woven from history and local character. Many Petersburgers are familiar with its magical effect: you have only to step onto its pavement and it catches you up and carries you along its masonry banks like a mysterious, never-stopping river of glittering lights. Like the Neva with its tributaries and side arms, Nevsky Prospekt with its adjoining streets and squares forms its own ensemble. Nevsky has many faces, many personalities, meanings, tones and memories – there are good reasons why since the early 19th-century days of Pushkin and the fable-writer Krylov each Petersburger has their own "Nevsky path", some special route unknown to others for getting from one point of personal importance to another. And although with the passing years the "stops" on and around Nevsky change for each of us, just as a anyone's tastes, needs, interests, passions and enthusiasms change, Nevsky Prospekt that has absorbed all our paths and crossings remains an unchanging and at the same time constantly changing river of life four and a half kilometres long.

The "Neva Perspective Road" first appeared back in Peter's time. It was flanked with birch trees and led from the Admiralty to the high road to Moscow and on to the Alexander Nevsky Monastery. It took centuries to become built up – here with mansions, there with palaces, elsewhere with average little houses with vegetable gardens behind them, and on the River Fontanka, where the city came to an end, you could go duck-hunting. It was not until the early 20th century that St Petersburg's main street finished acquiring a look that remains almost the same today. Together with its surviving traditional buildings in the Baroque and Neo-Classical styles, with churches of various confessions, palaces and bridges across three waterways, Nevsky Prospekt already bore traces of the new "Iron Age" (as it seemed then). They took the form of bank buildings, insurance companies, restaurants, glass fronts and other eccentricities of the modern era. Then it staunchly bore the imposition of the Communist name "Prospekt of 25 October". During the first siege winter of 1941-42 it came close to dying in the snow with the rest of the city, but then joyfully welcomed the victors home in 1945. At the end of the Soviet era it seemed lacklustre, stiff and grimy. And it is only now that it has once more come to look, as in the early 20th century, like the main street of a major European city with its day- and nightlife.

Looking westwards along Nevsky Prospekt towards the tower of the Admiralty

Looking eastwards along Nevsky Prospekt

The Stroganov Palace and the Singer Company Building

ONE façade of the Stroganov Palace stands on Nevsky Prospekt, the other on the embankment of the Moika. This spectacular building in the Baroque style was created by Francesco Bartolomeo Rastrelli in 1752–54 for one of Russia's richest families – the Stroganovs. Particularly famous among them was the enlightened aristocrat Alexander Stroganov (1733–1811), a well known patron of the arts and philanthropist, president of the Academy of Arts. His study in the palace has survived well, as have the Mineral Cabinet, the Picture Gallery, the Library and the Physics Cabinet. St Petersburg's leading artists worked on these interiors. The palace was a treasure-house of very rare paintings, sculpture, furniture and tableware – besides everything else the Stroganovs were superb connoisseurs of art and passionate collectors.

IN THE early 20th century Petersburgers devoted to tradition imagined that an irate Kutuzov standing on his pedestal before the Kazan Cathedral was waving his field marshal's baton at those who had dared to distort St Petersburg's classical appearance – the architects Alfred Parland with his Church of the Saviour on the Spilt Blood and Pavel Suzor, who in 1902–04 constructed an almost Chicago-school building for the American Singer sewing-machine company. Its tower of steel and glass in a style brazenly declared its novelty. The windows were exceptionally large thanks to the use of a steel-frame construction. Polished granite and wrought bronze spoke of the wealth of the client. The Stars and Stripes flew from the façade of the building as it housed the US consulate as well as foreign banks and offices. After the revolution, instead of banks and company offices its upper floors became home to Leningrad publishers and editorial offices, while the main rooms were taken by a book shop – the House of Books, another symbol of our city.

The Stroganov
Palace

The Great Hall
of the Stroganov
Palace

Nymphs with a
globe crowning
the cupola of the
House of Books

The House
of Books

The Kazan Cathedral

AT THE point where the Kazan Cathedral stands, Nevsky suddenly broadens out, forming an open space upon which the majestic colonnade of the Kazan Cathedral is arrayed in all its striking beauty. Paul I, under whom the cathedral was begun in 1801, intended it to copy the colonnade of St Peter's in Rome. The cathedral's architect, Andrei Voronikhin, was an astonishing man. One of Count Stroganov's serfs, he was endlessly grateful to his master, who not only helped him – a talented slave – to obtain a superb education in Russian and abroad, but also granted him his freedom and then continued to patronize his protégé, supplying him with commissions.

In 1811 Voronikhin's reward for the completion of the Kazan Cathedral was the Order of St Anne that gave him hereditary nobility. Voronikhin built many things in his lifetime, but the Kazan Cathedral, the swansong of an architect who died in 1814, immediately acquired a special place in the history and appearance of the capital. And although the praise of its architectural merits is sometimes exaggerated (it is after all no rival to Bramante and Michelangelo's tremendous creation in Rome), the symbolic importance of the Kazan Cathedral is exceptionally high. This place of worship, constructed from beginning to end by a Russian architect using local materials (Olonets marble, Pudost limestone, Serdobol granite) and decorated with sculpture by such outstanding Russian masters as Demuth-Malinovsky, Prokofiev, Martos and Stepan Pimenov, became in the period following Napoleon's invasion a new national sanctuary, a Russian Pantheon. It was here, in front of the Kazan Icon of the Virgin, that soldiers prayed before going off to fight the invader; here that trophy banners and the keys of cities taken by the Russian forces were brought. Here too in 1813 Mikhail Kutuzov, the heroic commander-in-chief of the "Patriotic War" was buried, and then Boris Orlovsky created monuments to him and another key figure of the war, Mikhail Barclay de Tolly, in front of the cathedral. In Soviet times the Kazan Cathedral was turned into a museum of atheism and it was only in the early 1990s that the cross was returned to its dome and its bells rang out anew. Today it is the main cathedral of St Petersburg.

The icon of the Virgin of Kazan, the main icon of the Kazan Cathedral

The tomb of Field Marshal Mikhail Kutuzov

The nave of the Kazan Cathedral with a view of the iconostasis

The Kazan
Cathedral

The monument
tof Field Marshal
Kutuzov

The north doors of
the cathedral and
statues of St Andrew
and John the Baptist

Bank Bridge

IF YOU stop for a moment on Kazan Bridge, which is even wider than Nevsky Prospekt itself and spans the Griboyedov Canal, formerly the Catherine Canal, then from one spot you get two very different, but memorable views: in one direction the celebrated Bank Bridge, in the other the Church of the Saviour on the Spilt Blood.

Bank Bridge is only a narrow pedestrian bridge with a wooden deck, one of many in St Petersburg, but this is no ordinary footbridge. Constructed over the Catherine Canal in 1826 to the design of the engineer Wilhelm von Traitteur, it is one of the few surviving St Petersburg chain suspension bridges. In this case the chains that support the bridge's 25-metre span run into the jaws of griffons. Of course, the chains are not really held in the teeth of these mythical creatures – they are anchored in a complex arrangement of iron rods hidden by their bodies and fixed in the granite abutments.

Griffons are among the most mysterious mythical entities. They come from the ancient East, Babylon and Assyria to be exact. Like the fabulous three-headed dogs, griffons tirelessly guarded hidden treasures. It is no coincidence that, thanks to the sculptor Pavel Sokolov, these griffons appeared on the banks of a peaceful St Petersburg canal. Firstly, according to the Ancient Greek historian Herodotus, griffons could be found in northern Europe, where there was "a great amount of gold" to be guarded from the thieving one-eyed Arimaspoi. Secondly, our griffons were placed in front of the Assignation Bank (hence the name of the bridge) to guard that institution which since Catherine II's time looked after the circulation of metal coins and paper money (assignation roubles). The building of the bank was completed in 1790 by the architect Giacomo Quarenghi. For more than a century this was the place to come to hear the clink of gold and silver – barges would pull up to the bank landing-stage and discharge their cargoes of coins in sacks that were then lugged to the bank's cellars. There was a time in the second half of the 19th century when it was decided to do away with the griffons and their footbridge, fill in the canal and turn it into a broad avenue. Fortunately a shortage of funding saved both the canal and the bridge with its fabulous beasts and today it often features along with St Petersburg's many other beauty spots in tourist brochures and guidebooks.

Bank Bridge

A griffon
on Bank Bridge

The Saviour on the Spilt Blood

IF A visitor from Moscow stands on Bank Bridge and looks into the distance across Nevsky Prospekt then it could well seem to him that during the night it took him to travel by train from the capital St Basil's Cathedral was brought from Moscow and set up on the canal in tight-laced northern St Petersburg. The Church of the Saviour on the Spilt Blood constructed on the bank of the Catherine Canal does indeed bear a great resemblance to the 16th-century Muscovite masterpiece with its multicoloured domes and distinctive arched gables.

It was built between 1883 and 1907 around that part of the granite embankment on which the blood of the mortally wounded Tsar Alexander II had been shed on 1 March 1881. Therefore the sacred centre of the church is a tent-roofed canopy resting on jasper columns between there is a cobbled section of the former roadway on which for decades the bloodstains remained visible.

At the time when this church-monument was built echoes of old Muscovy became fashionable. This was due to the ideology that prevailed in the reign of the murdered Tsar's successor, Alexander III (1881–1896), when there was an abrupt shift from the westward orientation of the period of Great Reforms to a search for Russia's own, special traditionally oriented course of development. Inevitably the "Russian Style" in all things found favour with the new Tsar and his court. It is not surprising, then, that the design for the Church of the Resurrection (the official name) inspired by 16th- and 17th-century Muscovite architecture that was put forward by the professional architect Alfred Parland and the churchman Archimandrite Ignaty (Malyshev) pleased Alexander III so much.

More than any other church in Russia the Saviour on the Spilt Blood is richly decorated with mosaics – the total area covered by the mosaic images is 7,000 square metres! The designs for the pictures were produced by outstanding artists of that time, including Victor Vasnetsov and Mikhail Nesterov. It was the incredible wealth of mosaics and tiles that enabled cultural activists in the Soviet period, when there was constant talk of the church's demolition, to stand up for it as an extremely valuable "museum of Russian mosaic". How fortunate for us. Approaching this splendid church glistening with all its colours in the sun that was constructed for such a tragic reason, we experience the same emotions that come over us during a church requiem service – sadness coupled with enlightenment and humility.

The mosaic of The *Crucifixion* on the west façade of the Saviour on the Spilt Blood

The railings of the Mikhailovsky Garden east of the Saviour on the Spilt Blood

The Church of the Saviour on the Spilt Blood (Church of the Resurrection)

Mosaics in the
vaults of the Saviour
on the Spilt Blood

The iconostasis

The mosaic depiction
of St Alexander Nevsky
in the iconostasis

The canopy above
the site of Alexander II's
assassination

The Tower of the City Duma and the Large Gostiny Dvor

THE tower of the City Duma is simply invaluable for Nevsky Prospekt as one of the vertical elements that articulate its architectural space.

The tower was erected by the Italian architect Giacomo Ferrari between 1799 and 1804. In 1824 a cabin for the optical telegraph was constructed on top of the upper tier of the tower. This was one of 149 stations that provided rapid communication over the immense distance from the Winter Palace to the Belweder in Warsaw. Later a metal construction was installed on the tower on which signal balls could be raised to inform Petersburgers of fires and their location in the city. Today the terracotta Duma tower is an inseparable part of Nevsky Prospekt and anyone walking along the street will inevitably take a glance at one of the three dials belonging to its unique tower clock, installed by Friedrich Winter in 1888 and still accurate to within half a minute a week. For many generations now the tower has served Petersburgers as a ready-made meeting point ("Let's meet by the Duma at six."). After all you can't possibly confuse it with anything else.

THE "shopping centre" known as the Large Gostiny Dvor is reckoned one of the city's first Neo-Classical buildings, after a change of reigns led to a sudden switch of architectural styles. In late December 1761 Empress Elizabeth passed away; then Peter III became Emperor for half a year before being ousted by Catherine II. Just as this change at the top occurred, Rastrelli completed his plans for a new Gostiny Dvor in the ornate Baroque style to replace the one lost to fire in 1737. To his chagrin Catherine gave preference to a different project – by Jean-Baptiste Vallin de La Mothe, who proposed a classically severe look for the building. His proposal was wholeheartedly supported by the merchants, because the budget for the Frenchman's project was far smaller – and they were the ones that would have to pay!

Vallin de La Mothe completed the construction of the Gostiny Dvor in 1785. From then on the Large Gostiny Dvor has been one of St Petersburg's major retail sites. Already in the early 1900s it was an association of different shops providing a high standard of service to customers who were for the most part privileged and wealthy. Gostiny Dvor was occupied by worthy trading houses with impeccable reputations, often purveyors to the imperial court.

Today it is again a shining cornucopia of goods offered by a variety of firms, including some of the world's leading names…

The Large Gostiny
Dvor

The tower of the
City Duma

The Square of Arts

A BROAD street running off Nevsky Prospekt provides a fine vista of the Mikhailovsky Palace. Although it long ago became home to the Russian Museum, the building still bears the name of its original owner – the professional soldier Grand Duke Mikhail Pavlovich, the youngest brother of Alexander I and Nicholas I. The palace, completed by Carlo Rossi in 1825, comes across as an ancient edifice standing on a non-existent hill. It is the organizing element for the whole ensemble of the square that originally bore the same name, but since 1940 has been the Square of the Arts. The new name is very apt. Besides the Russian Museum, it is also the location of the Mikhailovsky Theatre and the mansion (today's number 4/6) of Count Matvei Viyelgorsky, a passionate music-lover who played his Stradivarius cello to a professional standard. The "quartet gatherings" that he began expanded into concerts in which many great performers participated. His mansion is now a specialist school attached to the Russian Museum. But an even more celebrated centre of music in St Petersburg is the Philharmonic. Since 1921 it has occupied the building of the former Assembly of the Nobility constructed in 1839 to Rossi's design, like other buildings around the square. Its celebrated hall must have hosted well nigh all the greatest performers of the 20th century.

Credit is due to those architects who were tasked with building on Mikhailovsky Square after Rossi. They managed to sustain its classical style. This particularly applies to the Russian Ethnographic Museum with its glorious Marble Hall. This building, in the Russian Neo-Classical revival style, was put up in 1900–11 by the architect Vasily Svinyin. The same delicacy was displayed by Leonty Benois in his design for the extension to the Russian Museum now known as the Benois Wing, which was opened in 1919.

The oval Mikhailovsky Garden was laid out in the centre of the square in 1827–28, again planned by Rossi. Today it is a wonderful miniature park with almost 200 trees, elms, oaks, maples and limes, and a host of Hungarian lilac bushes.

The Square of the Arts ensemble acquired its final form in 1957, when the monument to Russia's national poet, Alexander Pushkin, designed by Mikhail Anikushin was installed in the centre. The exquisite depiction of the poet reciting his verse put the final seal on this little corner of St Petersburg, giving it finished perfection.

The building of
the Ethnographic
Museum

The monument
to Alexander
Pushkin

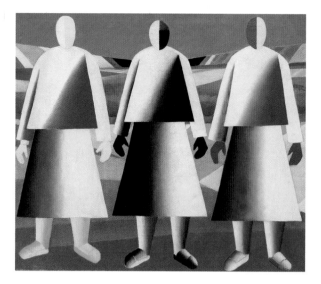

The Russian Museum

THANKS to the support of the imperial family, the Russian Museum, which opened in 1898, rapidly became one of the largest collections of the nation's art in many manifestations: painting, sculpture, graphic art, decorative and applied art (from furniture to lace). The museum's stocks are said to number at least 400,000 items.

People come here specially to see the incomparable beauty of early Russian icons of the 12th–14th centuries, some the work of unknown masters, others by such famous names as Andrei Rublev, Dionysius and Simon Ushakov. They stop in reverence before the unusual icon of *The Angel with the Golden Hair,* the *Virgin of Tenderness* (late 14th century) or *St George and the Dragon* (14th–15th century).

Nowhere in the world is there such a full collection of Russian paintings and sculpture from the 18th century and first half of the 19th, including works by artists of Peter I's time (Andrei Matveyev, Ivan Nikitin). of the heyday of Classical art (Vladimir Borovikovsky, Anton Losenko, Dmitry Levitsky, Fedot Shubin and others), of Russian Romanticism and Realism (Orest Kiprensky, Vasily Vereshchagin, Karl Briullov, Alexander Ivanov, Alexei Venetsianov, Pavel Fedotov). Still today, as in the 19th century, visitors crowd around Briullov's painting of *The Last Day of Pompeii* that in its time caused a furore in Europe. On a par with the Classical collection are the works of the "Itinerants" from the second half of the 19th century Ivan Shishkin, Ivan Kramskoi, Ilya Repin, Victor Vasnetsov, Vasily Surikov and many others). In the Soviet period the museum staff selflessly defied the dominant ideology and aesthetics of "Socialist Realism" to save from destruction the works of Kazimir Malevich and other members of the Russian avant-garde. Now their paintings, along with those of such famous groupings as the World of Art, the Blue Rose and the Jack of Diamonds are an adornment of the Russian Museum.

The icon of
*The Angel with
the Golden Hair*

Kazimir Malevich.
Girls in a Field

The portico of
the Mikhailovsky
Palace

The Main Staircase
of the Mikhailovsky
Palace

The White Hall
(State Drawing-
Room)

The Academic
(Briullov) Hall

The portal with
caryatids

The display of
sculpture and
painting from the
first half of the
19th century

Ostrovsky Square

IN 1801, on the corner of Nevsky Prospekt and Sadovaya Street, the architect Yegor Sokolov erected for the Public Library (now the National Library of Russia) a building whose rounded façade has adorned that junction ever since. That building became the starting point for an urban reconstruction project carried out by Carlo Rossi in the 1820s and early 1830s.

He began by creating two exquisite pavilions in the garden of the Anichkov Palace. Later he extended the building of the Public Library, investing it with features of a temple of learning. The majestic columns seem to part in order to provide space for statues of great philosophers, scholars and poets. From the attic storey the goddess of wisdom Minerva extends her protection to them all.

In 1832 Rossi constructed the Alexandrinsky Theatre, named in honour of Empress Alexandra Feodorovna, the consort of Emperor Nicholas I. Behind the theatre Rossi created a unique street that in 1923 was renamed in honour of the architect who gave it "ideal" proportions – its width is equal to the height of the buildings (22 metres), while its length is ten times the width. Not a single photographer (whether in the 19th century or the 21st) can pass this wonder by – Carlo Rossi, the wizard of true measure and divine proportions, created a masterpiece that triggers an urge to shoot it in spring and autumn, in the rains and the snow, at dawn and at dusk, by day and by night.

The square in front of the theatre was also called after Empress Alexandra, until in 1923 it was given the name of the dramatist Alexander Ostrovsky. In 1873 a monument to Catherine II by the sculptor Mikhail Mikeshin was set up here. The figure of the Tsarina rises from a pedestal that is surrounded by nine of her closest associates. It is a fine piece of work not so much for its artistic qualities as for its entertainment value: for almost a century and a half now, beneath the lazy gaze of locals half-reclining on the benches, curious tourists have been making a circuit of it: they simply have to view all the figures and read the inscriptions beneath them. With its fresh shady greenery the garden that now surrounds the monument has become a charming quiet backwater into which one can escape from the noisy torrent of Nevsky Prospekt.

The Yeliseyevs' shop

The façade of the Public Library from Ostrovsky Square

Ostrovsky Square with a view of the Alexandrinsky Theatre and the monument to Catherine II

Anichkov Bridge

ANICHKOV Bridge spans the River Fontanka and got its name from a Captain Mikhail Anichkov, whose engineering battalion built the original bridge here in 1715. In 1841–42, during a radical reconstruction of the bridge (not the first) someone came up with the idea of putting on the pedestals at its corners the statues of the Horse-Tamers that Peter Klodt had produced to decorate the landing stage by the Academy of Arts. Their place there was taken by the Egyptian sphinxes, and the horses were "banished" to Nevsky Prospekt. The first two sculptures were installed on the west side of the bridge. Two more, repeating these, were unexpectedly presented by Nicholas I to King Frederick William IV of Prussia. When Klodt cast the sculptures again, the Emperor gave those away as well, in 1846, to the King of the Two Sicilies It was only in 1851 that this equestrian tale came to an end, when two more sculptures were installed on the bridge, but new, original ones. As a result, thanks to the Emperor's extravagance and the sculptor's creative imagination, the Anichkov Bridge acquired an exceptional sculptural ensemble devoted to man's taming of the horse – an allegory of harnessing the forces of nature.

A striking background for this ensemble is provided by the Beloselsky-Belozersky Palace that acquired its present appearance in 1847–48, when the architect Andrei Stakenschneider took it in hand. Working in the Neo-Baroque style he created a striking red-walled palace with two facades of equal status, on the Fontanka and on Nevsky Prospekt.

North of the bridge, behind dense railings with a gilded coat-of-arms above the central wrought-iron gates, stands an authentic Baroque edifice, the Sheremetev Palace, created as we see it now by Savva Chevakinsky in the mid-1700s. Since 1712 the site was the main St Petersburg residence of Field Marshal Boris Sheremetev, a close associate of Peter I, and it remained in the family until 1917. The interiors of the palace were repeatedly refurbished to keep up with fashion by three generations of Sheremetevs. The family were passionately fond of music, kept their own choir and organized concerts by leading musicians. The elaborate wrought-iron railing was created by the architect Ieronimo Corsini in 1838.

One of the *Horse-Tamer* sculptures with the Beloselsky-Belozersky Palace in the background

The Anichkov Bridge

The Sheremetev Palace

St Michael's Castle

THE majestic building that stands close to the Field of Mars and the Summer Garden is known as St Michael's Castle from its church dedicated to the Archangel Michael. Emperor Paul I, who came to power in 1796, felt uncomfortable in the residences used by his mother, Catherine II, and so he decided to have a completely new palace constructed for himself that would reflect ideas that he cherished and his aesthetic tastes. That is how the Emperor, who saw himself as a chivalrous knight, produced a residence imitating the strongholds of mediaeval Europe, surrounded by ramparts and moats. It has now been established that besides the architect Vincenzo Brenna, who directed construction, Paul himself was heavily involved in designing the building. The castle was built between 1797 and 1801 and the Tsar directed enormous resources to the project – up to 6,000 workers that he ordered to labour unceasingly, even at night by the light of torches and lamps.

In front of the castle Paul set up Carlo Bartolomeo Rastrelli's equestrian statue of Peter the Great from the 1740s that Catherine II had disliked and kept in a shed. On the pedestal of the monument that was inaugurated in 1801 he had words placed that were clearly meant as a riposte to the inscription on the Bronze Horseman: "To great-grandfather from great-grandson". Although the decoration of the palace-castle was still not finished in early 1801 and the rooms were still damp, Paul moved into his new home and took his family with him. But he lived in the castle for just forty days. On the night of 11 March 1801 he was killed in his own bedroom by conspirators from the Guards officer corps. There is a legend that a few months before the Emperor's death a holy fool appeared in St Petersburg who predicted that the Tsar would live as many years as there were letters in the inscription above the entrance to the new palace. This was a biblical quotation, "Holiness becometh thine house, O Lord, for ever," that contained forty-seven Russian letters. Paul was indeed assassinated in his forty-seventh year. After his death the palace was abandoned until in 1823 it was given over to the college of military engineers (hence the second name – Engineers' Castle). The rebirth of the palace began in the early 1990s and today the near-impossible has been accomplished: St Michael's Castle now looks much as it did in Paul's time.

View of St Michael's Castle from the entrance to the Summer Garden

The monument to Peter I in front of the castle's south facade

St Michael's Castle

The Summer Garden

WHAT we now call the Summer Garden was known in Peter I's own time as "the Summer Court". Here, where the River Fontanka flows out of the Neva, from 1703 stood Peter's first Summer Palace, that in 1711 seemed to a foreign traveller "a little house… built in the Dutch style". In 1714 the second Summer Palace, which has survived to this day, was constructed on the same site. The origin of the name is quite interesting. The age-old Muscovite tradition of the Tsar moving out of the Kremlin for the summer to a residence in the suburbs was carried over to St Petersburg, although here the Summer Palace was located just a kilometre up the Neva from the Winter Palace. Today the Summer Palace houses a museum with a large number of items from Peter I's time and a visit there will help to understand and appreciate many things about the extraordinary life story of Russia's great reformer.

The palace stood in a garden of which Peter was extremely fond. It was laid out in accordance with all the rules of Dutch park design: with trimmed trees and bushes, fountains, ponds, a menagerie, a grotto and sculpture from Italy. Peter devoted every free minute to the garden, sparing nothing to decorate his "backyard". In his time the garden was a place for the Tsar's family and guests to relax in. Later it was opened to visitors as well. Between 1771 and 1784 Yury Veldten erected a railing on the Neva side of the garden that has become one of the sights of St Petersburg.

A terrible flood in 1777 devastated the Summer Garden and it was restored to its former "regular" appearance only very recently. It has now regained Baroque fountains, a menagerie and other amusements of Peter's time.

One of the enduring attractions of the Summer Garden is the 1855 monument to the Russian fable-writer Ivan Krylov. This work by Piotr Klodt may seem eclectic to us today; the high reliefs attached to its base overcrowded with the personages of Krylov's fables, but that is not important – it is so interesting to look at and identify them. "Grandfather Krylov" is a general favourite. Under his benevolent gaze generation after generation of little Petersburgers have wagged their fingers at the terrible wolf or laughed at the stupid crow that dropped the cheese from its beak, and then grown up to bring their own children to see Krylov.

The Neva-side
railings of the
Summer Garden

The Summer
Palace of Peter I

The *Crown* fountain

A green alley

The monument
to Ivan Krylov

The Field of Mars

EVEN in the early 20th century, despite its size and its central location, the Field of Mars was not really a square but more of an actual open field. On ordinary days it was deserted. In summer the wind raised clouds of dust which inspired the locals to call it "the St Petersburg Sahara". In winter the Field of Mars became a snowy wasteland with drifts transected by narrow paths stamped out by people eager to get across this unpleasant exposed expanse of white as quickly as possible. But the Field of Mars was not always a lifeless Sahara or an empty plain of snow. On this area, originally known as the Tsarina's Meadow, Peter I held parades of the Guards on special occasions and here too he treated that elite of his army to a traditional cup of vodka. In Empress Elizabeth's time the place was called the Promenade; citizens strolled its avenues that had been planted with trees and bushes and sometimes could be seen crowding after the elephant from the menagerie that had also been brought out for a walk.

From 1805 Tsarina's Meadow began to be called the Field of Mars and it became the setting for famous parades. These events customarily attracted huge numbers of spectators who watched with great excitement as the redoubtable infantry regiments marched by to the accompaniment of the regimental bands and dashing cavalrymen controlled their steeds at the gallop. Perhaps the Field of Mars's acquisition of such a warlike character was connected with the fact that in 1798–1801 the first monuments were set up here to two military commanders who had won glory in the wars against Turkey in the second half of the 18th century: the obelisk to Field Marshal Piotr Rumiantsev (architect: Vincenzo Brenna) and the monument to Alexander Suvorov (sculptor: Mikhail Kozlovsky). In 1818 the Rumiantsev Obelisk was transferred to Vasilyevsky Island, while the Suvorov Monument was shifted closer to where the Trinity Bridge now crosses the Neva. This was done because the memorials had been interfering with the parades. In time the snow-covered Field of Mars became the setting for great popular festivities at Shrovetide with swings, ice slides, a circus and a host of sideshows. In the revolutionary era a memorial was created in the middle of the Field of Mars and by it they started to bury people who had been killed in the fighting in Petrograd and elsewhere.

The Eternal Flame on the Field of Mars

The monument to Generalissimo Suvorov

The monument to Emperor Alexander III in the courtyard of the Marble Palace

The Field of Mars

Vasilyevsky Island

AT THE city's foundation Vasilyevsky Island was a huge expanse of boreal forest. So it remained until 1715, when after long consideration Peter decided to construct the centre of his capital on the island. The Tsar approved the plan for its development drawn up by Trezzini and even personally pegged out the general direction of the "lines" that were not to be streets in the usual sense, but the banks of parallel canals to be dug out from the Large Neva into the heart of the island. The prototype for the new project was Peter's beloved Amsterdam. The Tsar dreamt of a day when he would be able to travel by boat around quiet canals past a solid wall of multi-coloured houses like in the Dutch capital.

But sadly this was not destined to be – all that remains of Peter's project are the numbered lines, converted into streets that intersect with three larger "still-born" canals – the island's Bolshoi, Sredny and Maly Prospekts. The focal point of the island became not the square, which never was constructed, but the famous Spit of Vasilyevsky Island adorned by a distinctive architectural ensemble.

The heart of the ensemble on the headland is our "northern Parthenon" – the building of the Exchange, constructed by Thomas de Thomon in 1810. It rises from a majestic pedestal and its huge white Doric columns draw the eye, as do the unusual red pillar towers in front of the building – the Rostral Columns that were constructed at the same time. The columns are decorated with rostra – the symbolic prows of captured enemy ships, while seated comfortably enthroned at their bases are four figures representing the Rivers Neva, Volga, Dnieper and Volkhov. The Rostral Columns were not only decorative, but functional – the signal fires lit at their tops could be seen from quite a distance. From 1727 until the middle of the 19th century the Spit served as the city's port and ships flying the flags of dozens of countries lay in several rows along the banks of the Small Neva. This was a noisy, bustling place like any port in the world.

The port also extended down the Large Neva, alongside the Exchange's southern warehouse. Today that massive building contains the Zoological Museum, a favourite with St Petersburg's children.

Further down the Neva, along University Embankment, stand buildings that brought Russia fame as a place in which science and education were highly esteemed. The green

The Spit of
Vasilyevsky Island

and white building with a tower embellished with a copper globe is the Kunstkammer – the first Russian museum, instituted by Peter in 1718. Next to the Kunstkammer stands the edifice of the Academy of Sciences, constructed in 1789 by that magician of Neo-Classicism Giacomo Quarenghi. The building of the Twelve Collegia is unique for both its length (the corridor stretches for 400 metres!) and the history of its construction. Peter's plan to concentrate all the central institutions of the state in one place required enormous efforts. On the site where this smart-looking building now stands, several thousand piles, up to 8 metres long, were driven into the ground – not just around the perimeter but everywhere, forming a solid unbroken platform. In 1818 the building of the Twelve Collegia became home to St Petersburg University.

A real gem of University Embankment is the Menshikov Palace (1710), created by the architects Fontana and Schädel. The owner of the edifice, Peter I's favourite, Alexander Menshikov, made himself such a luxurious residence that the Tsar himself used it to receive ambassadors and for official celebrations. In the last twenty years it has become a wonderful museum devoted to Russian 18th-century culture.

The site of the Academy of Arts was once occupied by the building of the first Russian drama theatre. It was opened in 1756 by Empress Elizabeth, a passionate theatre-goer, but in the mid-1760s the theatre was demolished and work began on the Academy of Arts, designed by Alexander Kokorinov and Jean-Baptiste Vallin de La Mothe. The founding father and long-time curator of the Academy of Arts (established in 1757) was Empress Elizabeth's favourite, Ivan Shuvalov, an educated, intelligent man. He invited experienced educators from Europe and made journeys to Italy compulsory for graduates. He himself lived abroad for a long time and constantly sent back works of art to his beloved academy.

Griffon on the Sphinxes Landing-Stage by the Academy of Arts during a flood

From the tall windows of the academy there is a striking view of the broad Neva, the opposite bank with the dome of St Isaac's and the spire of the Admiralty, the majestic Annunciation Bridge and, in the foreground, a granite landing-stage on which stand two granite sphinxes from Thebes staring straight at one another.

The ensemble
on the Spit of
Vasilyevsky Island

The granite
landing-stage
of the Spit

A statue at
the foot of the
northern Rostral
Column

A Rostral
Column

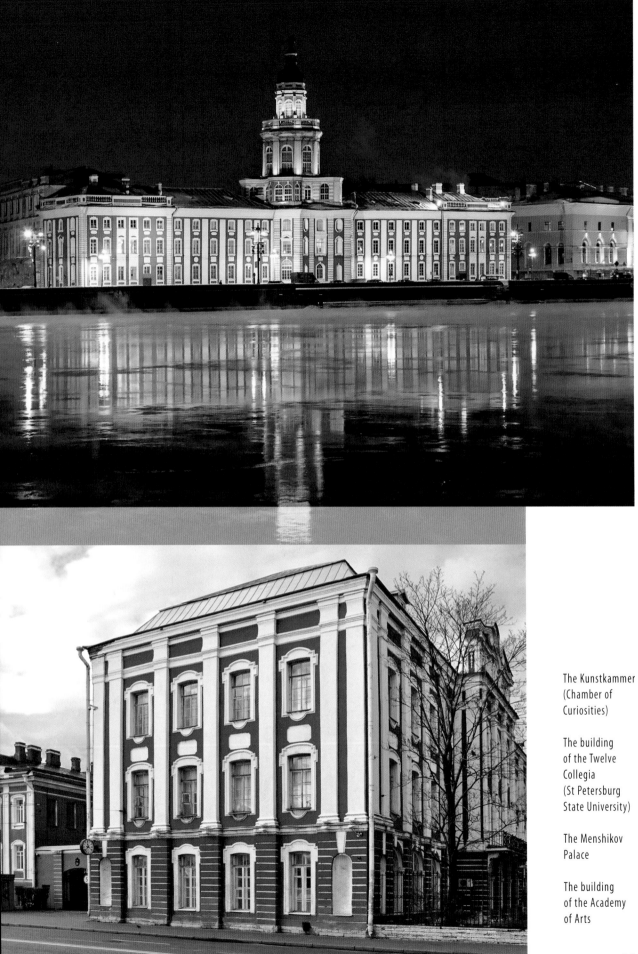

The Kunstkammer
(Chamber of
Curiosities)

The building
of the Twelve
Collegia
(St Petersburg
State University)

The Menshikov
Palace

The building
of the Academy
of Arts

The sphinxes
in front of the
Academy of Arts

The Venice of the North

THE Neva and Peter the Great between them created St Petersburg. It was not for nothing that the poet Bulat Okudzhava called the city's main river "Neva Petrovna", the patronymic stressing their kinship. It proved very important for St Petersburg's classical appearance that the river is very broad, stately and majestic, with a wealth of side arms – the Fontanka, Moika and Griboyedov Canal that make the magic of this exceptional city.

Only the broad expanse of the Neva, though, makes it possible to truly appreciate the brilliant creations of its architects. Anyone on the banks one can see the grandeur of St Petersburg's architecture, its inseparability from the spaciousness of the river. The Neva integrates the city into a single grand whole, gives St Petersburg an exceptional landscape quality. And this urban landscape on the river is just as much a monument to be carefully preserved as any historical building.

Between the Winter Palace, the Spit of Vasilyevsky Island and the Peter and Paul Fortress the Neva turns into a huge watery "square". Framed by the bridges and the horizontal lines of the embankments, marked out by verticals of the Rostral Columns, the SS Peter and Paul Cathedral and the Admiralty needle, this "square" enables us to embrace the whole grand panorama with a sweeping glance.

Smoothly and unobtrusively this "watery square" flows into the chain of man-made squares on the left bank of the Neva: the Field of Mars, Suvorov, Palace, Senate and St Isaac's Squares, forming a single ensemble of open air-filled urban spaces, demonstrating the unity between the creation of humans and nature. A 19th-century French traveller accustomed to the cramped architectural cosiness of Paris found these squares "wastelands surrounded by low buildings". For us locals, though, this ensemble of squares is an architectural symbol of the great Russian Empire with its boundless plains lying beneath the high dome of the Russian sky. And still today each of us clearly understands when we stand on Palace Embankment by the Winter Palace that that granite fringe of the Admiralty Side in St Petersburg marks the start of a landmass that extends for a week's journey on the ground, many hours by air, to the shoreline at Vladivostok – our immense homeland, mighty Russia.

The Neva is especially beautiful in the White Nights of summer, when dusk merges into dawn. At that time you understand especially plainly that the unbroken fusion of

Ships on the
Large Neva

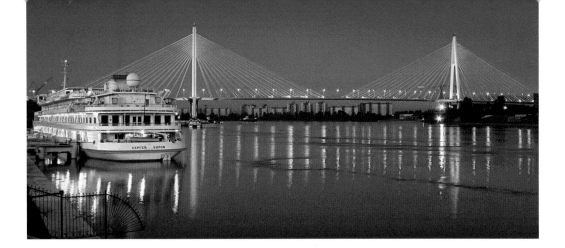

architecture and nature, city and river, the astonishing combination of delicate north-ern colours and hues has its own depth, clarity and watercolour exquisiteness. The thin needle of the Admiralty burns in the rays of a sun unseen beyond the horizon. Its bright gold contests with the heavier shade on the massive dome of St Isaac's that seems to hang above the Neva, while the emerald green of the Alexander Garden combines in an astonishing way with the turquoise of the Baroque Winter Palace and the age-old patina of the Bronze Horseman.

A wealth of different shades of green set off the dandified neatness of Rossi's and Zakharov's yellow and white creations – the General Staff, Senate and Admiralty. Be-neath the pale Petersburg sky the buildings on the embankments seem to be viewing themselves in the pearly-grey Neva. At such moments one calls to mind the compari-sons between St Petersburg and some harmonious chorus. And since a great many musical masterpieces and great works of poetry have been written on these banks, it seems especially in the White Nights that the very city is filled with the sounds of divine music and marvellous verses.

Once a year, when the school-leaving examinations are over, thousands of teenag-ers gather on the banks of the Neva one bright night and the city puts on the glorious celebration of the "Scarlet Sails" for them.

The Neva is a navigable river and by night dozens of vessels travel up and down it. To allow them through, the bridges on the Neva in the city are raised: Annunciation, Palace, Trinity, Liteiny, Bolsheokhtinsky, Alexander Nevsky and Volodarsky Bridges, as well as two on the Small Neva – Exchange and Tuchkov. This, one might think, purely technical process becomes a fascinating spectacle which many people – locals and visitors – line the banks of the Neva specially to see. The gigantic spans of the bridges raised into the sky, the lights and hooters of the huge vessels that crawl slowly between the piers of each bridge – all of it reflected and sparkling in the oily, dark-blue surface of the Neva, turns everything taking place on the river into a colourful, unforgettable per-formance. At such moments you inevitably wonder what St Petersburg's great founder would have said on witnessing this extraordinary sight. He would probably have shout-ed out: "Vivat! Well done!" His dream has come true.

Panorama of the Neva with a view of the Large Obukhovsky Bridge

The landing-stage on the Spit of Vasilyevsky Island during a flood

Palace Landing-Stage on Admiralty Embankment

A regatta on the Large Neva

The railing of the Annunciation Bridge

A panorama of the River Fontanka

Bridges over the Fontanka (with Lomonosov Bridge in the foreground)

The junction of the Kriukov and Griboyedov Canals with a view of the St Nicholas Cathedral ensemble

Palace Bridge
raised

Bolsheokhtinsky
Bridge

The Neva during
the Scarlet Sails
festival

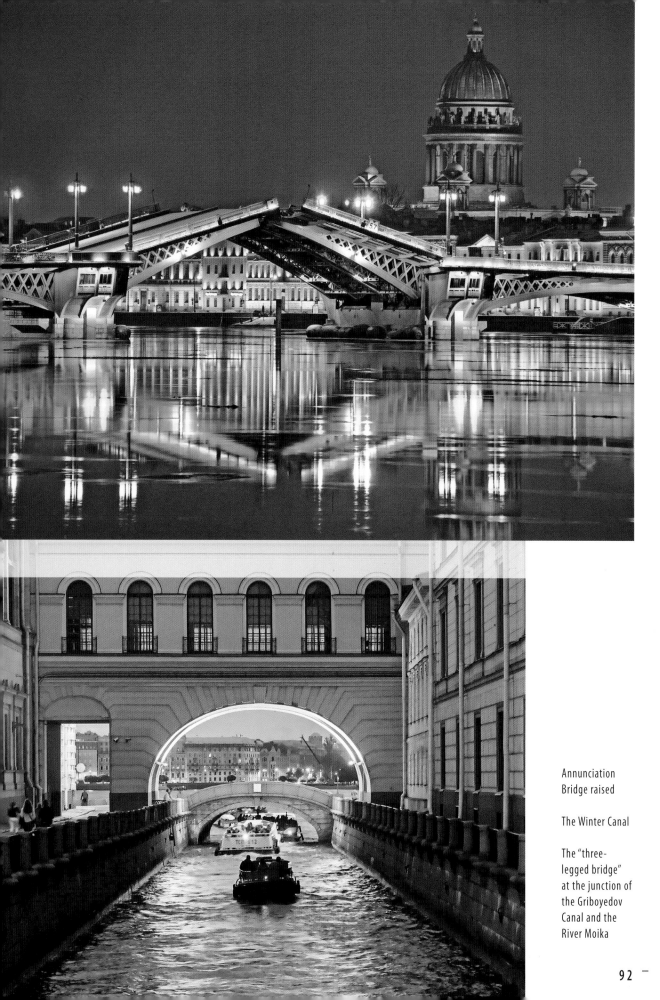

Annunciation
Bridge raised

The Winter Canal

The "three-
legged bridge"
at the junction of
the Griboyedov
Canal and the
River Moika

Theatre Square and its Surroundings

IN THE 18th century the western part of Admiralty Island was a sort of support area for the Admiralty shipyard. Employees of the Naval Department lived here (in Empress Elizabeth's time the architect Savva Chevakinsky built the St Nicolas Naval Cathedral for them) and there were sawmills that produced timber for ships. The wood was floated along canals to the store of New Holland, a facility established by Peter I and reconstructed under Catherine II by Chevakinsky and Vallin de La Mothe, who turned this complex of functional buildings into one of the most romantic sights of St Petersburg. Here to, along the Moika, an aristocratic suburb formed with a string of rich urban estates. Their unusual proximity to one of the oldest working-class districts gives this area, which retains its layout from the 1730s, a distinctive St Petersburg character. Its poetry lies not only in the narrow streets and lanes, but also in the rivers and canals winding between the areas of housing, spanned by picturesque bridges reflected in the dark, slow-moving waters. Houses on the banks of these waterways are associated with Pushkin, Dostoyevsky, Leo Tolstoy, Tchaikovsky, Mussorgsky, Glinka, Blok, Repin, Stravinsky, the World of Art artists and many others who lived or worked here, creating masterpieces that brought fame to the Russian arts. A reminder of the aristocratic thread in the area's history is the Yusupov Palace, the St Petersburg residence of an extremely wealthy princely family. Its unimpressive exterior conceals sumptuous rooms including a domestic theatre for an audience of 180. Tat theatre is like a miniature version of the Mariinsky, the most famous building on Theatre Square. It was created by the architect Albert Cavos in the reign of Alexander II and named in honour of Empress Maria Alexandrovna. It opened on 2 October 1860 and soon became the centre of Russian opera and ballet. Those who sung here included Sobinov and Chaliapin; Petipa and Fokine staged ballets danced by legendary figures, including Anna Pavlova and Nijinsky.

The New Holland arch

The Mariinsky Theatre

The interior of the Mariinsky Theatre

The interior of the theatre in the Yusupov Palace

The Capital of All Religions

FROM the very outset St Petersburg was created as a secular, multi-confessional, cosmopolitan city, open to people of all religions. That was done deliberately. In order to attract the specialist that he needed from abroad, Peter accepted a relaxation of the traditional Muscovite religious intolerance. There had probably never been a capital like this before, with churches of non-native confessions constructed in the very centre. First to be "legitimized" in St Petersburg was the Lutheran community, for whom a small wooden Church of St Anne (1704) was built inside the Peter and Paul Fortress. The first mention of a Catholic congregation comes not much later (in 1710 Peter I became godfather to the son of his Catholic architect Domenico Trezzini). That same year the court gardener Peter van der Gaar donated a plot of land in the Greek settlement (Millionnaya Street) for the construction of the city's first Catholic church. At the same time Peter wanted his beloved city to become a focus of the Orthodox faith and did much to that end, Churches were erected in all parts of the city and in 1710 he founded the Alexander Nevsky Monastery. In 1723 Peter gave orders for the relics of that sainted prince, who in 1240 had won a victory in these parts over the Swedes as Peter had done in 1703. In July 1763 Catherine II issued a manifesto permitting all peoples settled in Russia to practise their religious rites. In both capitals places were set aside for non-Orthodox churches. Masonry Catholic and Armenian churches were erected on Nevsky Prospekt. The expansion of the empire in the 19th century and the annexation of new territories brought a need for places of worship for other religions in the capital. Alexander III permitted the construction of the first synagogue. Nicholas II's reign saw the building of a mosque and a Buddhist temple. So by the beginning of the 20th century St Petersburg had become a place where all the world's major religions – Christianity, Judaism, Islam and Buddhism – were represented.

The Trinity Cathedral of the Alexander Nevsky Monastery

The interior of the Trinity Cathedral of the Alexander Nevsky Monastery with a view of the iconostasis

Smolny
Cathedral of the
Resurrection

The St Nicholas
Naval Cathedral

The Trinity
Izmailovsky
Cathedral

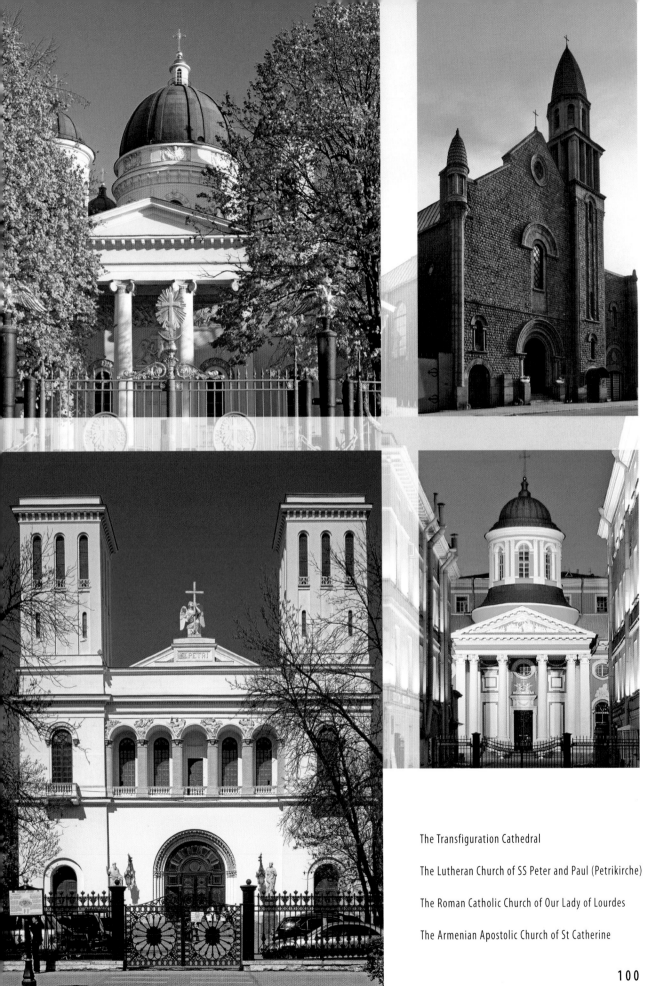

The Transfiguration Cathedral

The Lutheran Church of SS Peter and Paul (Petrikirche)

The Roman Catholic Church of Our Lady of Lourdes

The Armenian Apostolic Church of St Catherine

The Church of the Nativity of St John the Baptist (Chesme Church)

The Buddhist temple, Küntsé-choinéi datsan

The Great Choral Synagogue

The Congregational Mosque

Victory monuments

FROM the outset St Petersburg was not only the political capital of Russia, but also its military capital, where the best architects and sculptors celebrated Russia's wartime triumphs in stone and bronze. Founded as a Russian advance-post in the Northern war (1700–21), from 1703 onwards the city marked victories of Russian arms on a grand scale – the St Peter Gate of the fortress, churches consecrated to saints on whose days this or that battle was won, the tremendous fountain ensemble at Peterhof. In Catherine II's time, when Neo-Classicism flourished, military memorials acquired a look more familiar to us today – obelisks and columns. There are especially many of these in Tsarskoye Selo, where the Empress perpetuated the memory of every each Russian victory in the Russo-Turkish Wars. After Napoleon was driven out of Russian in 1812, St Petersburg was embellished with majestic triumphal arches in the style of the Roman Empire – the arch of the General Staff on Palace Square, the Moscow and Narva Gates are symbols of the Russian martial spirit. The celebrated Alexander Column is also a monument to the victory of 1812. In the early 20th century Russia experienced two conflicts – the Russo-Japanese War and the First World War. While the former was commemorated, despite the defeat, in the monument to the torpedo boat *Steregushchy*, for example, the latter became a forgotten war in Leningrad, as the Bolsheviks renamed the city. In-dividual monuments (the Hero-City obelisk by the Moscow Railway Station and others) are devoted to the siege (1941–44) and defence of Leningrad during the Second World War as are whole memorial complexes: the Monument to the Heroic Defenders of Len-ingrad on the square at the end of Moscow Prospekt and the Piskarevskoye Memorial Cemetery, both of which are also museums.

The Moscow Gate

The Narva Gate

The Monument
to the Heroic
Defenders of
Leningrad

Peterhof

IT IS impossible to picture St Petersburg without its magnificent suburban residences, among which a special place is occupied by Peterhof, first recorded in 1705. By roughly 1710 Peter had settled on a plan for the ensemble that took account of the distinctive character of the terrain: a flat shore that ends in a tall ridge. Peter jotted on a piece of paper that still survives a diagram showing a palace on the hill (the "Upper Chambers") and three radial lines running from it. They represented the Sea Canal and two broad avenues – the basis of the "geometry" that gave the whole ensemble its exceptional orderliness, simplicity and elegance.

The Lower Park is the chief element of the Peterhof ensemble, its true gem. It occupies the whole area between the shore of the Gulf of Finland and the terrace with the Great Cascade and Great Palace, from which avenues lead to three lesser palaces – Monplaisir, Marly and the Hermitage.

The Great Palace soars above the park harmoniously beautiful. It was begun in Peter's time, but it acquired its present magnificence as a result of Rastrelli's work in the mid-18th century. It contains a sumptuous suite of thirty halls and rooms richly decorated with gilded woodcarving, stucco, paintings and mirrors.

The Lower Park owes its special charm to its many and varied fountains. Water descends down the Chessboard Hill and Golden Hill cascades and spurts upwards in the Roman Fountains, the inventive Pyramid, Sun and Ménager Fountains and the amusing trick fountains. The creators of the park made sure that visitors hear the "play of water", a whole liquid symphony: the thunder of a waterfall, the roar of a mountain spring, the murmur of springtime rivulets…

But the grandest and most magnificent of all the Peterhof's hydraulic installations has always been the Great Cascade and, at its foot, the "king" of the Peterhof fountains – *Samson Tearing Open the Jaws of the Lion.*

The Great
Peterhof Palace

The *Samson
Tearing Apart the
Jaws of the Lion*
fountain

The Ballroom of the Great
Peterhof Palace

The Main Staircase

The Eastern Chinese
Cabinet

The Chessboard Hill
cascade

The *Sun* fountain

The *Eve* fountain

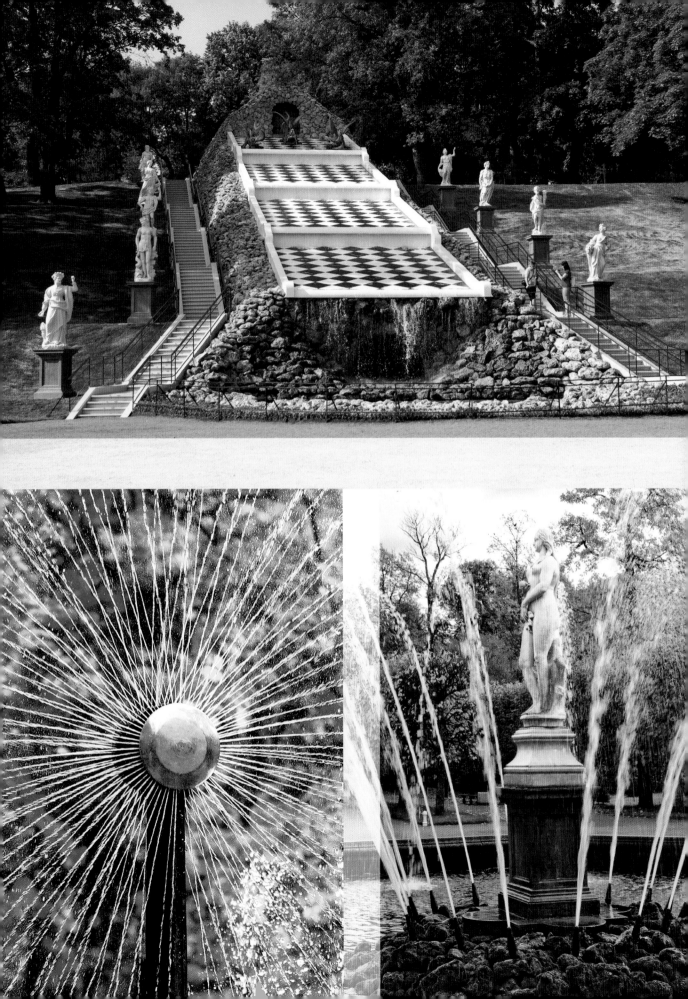

Oranienbaum

AS HE constructed and beautified his own suburban residences, Peter the Great encouraged his close associates to do the same. As a result rich manors sprang up along the shores of the Gulf of Finland. Particularly notable among them was the coastal estate of Peter's right-hand man, Alexander Menshikov, who built himself a truly princely residence at Oranienbaum. Its main edifice was the Great (Menshikov) Palace that was built between 1710 and 1725 by the architects Fontana and Schädel. The Lower Garden was laid out in front of the palace; while behind lay a splendid park with a pond hothouses and a menagerie.

The Oranienbaum park contains one more real gem – the Chinese Palace, a wonder among Russian architecture. It was constructed by Antonio Rinaldi for Empress Catherine II in 1762–68. Rinaldi was also the creator of the Coasting Hill complex from 1774 from which the blue and white pavilion has survived and impresses everyone with its harmonious proportions. From it half-kilometre-long tracks once descended with three intermediate rises. In 1801 they were dismantled, but the long attractive meadow through which they ran still exists, fringed as before with tall dark firs.

The Great
Menshikov Palace

The Hall of the
Muses in the
Chinese Palace

The Coasting-Hill
Pavilion

Tsarskoye Selo

IN 1710 Peter I presented the manor of Sarskaya (a name that evolved into Tsarskoye Selo – "Tsar's Village") to his wife, Catherine. In the 1730s, when Anna Ioannovna was on the throne, Peter and Catherine's daughter Elizabeth spent much of her time in this then-remote suburb, avoiding the persistent surveillance of the Empress's spies. Tsarskoye Selo really began to flourish when Elizabeth herself came to the throne. A leading role was played by her architect Rastrelli. When he finished his work, it was received with boundless delight. Those approaching Tsarskoye Selo were suddenly met by a glorious sight: against a background of blue sky and green forest the royal palace shone in the sun – many of the Baroque decorative elements on the facades were covered with gold. And gleaming above them all were the gold domes of the court church. But what visitors encountered on entering the palace was stunning. After passing through a succession of antechambers with paintings on the ceilings, parquet floors of rare kinds of wood and gilded woodcarving, guests reached the Great Hall – the palace's main architectural treasure. A fantastically beautiful floor, huge windows interspersed with mirrors, gilded carving everywhere and the whole beneath a tremendous ceiling painting by the artist Giuseppe Valeriani. The greatest of all the palace's wonders was reckoned to be the Amber Room, whose walls were transformed by panels assembled from pieces of amber and mosaic pictures. Catherine II preferred Tsarskoye Selo among all the suburban residences. In her time it was enriched by the Cameron Gallery, built in 1784–87 to the design of the British architect Charles Cameron, and many monuments appeared in the park to mark Russian victories over the Ottoman Empire, as well as elegant pavilions and amusing chinoiserie structures.

Tsarskoye Selo is dear to every Russian's heart, because a wing built on to the palace in the 1790s housed the Imperial Lyceum, a boarding school for noble boys in which Alexander Pushkin spent his childhood and youth from 1811. The Lyceum garden contains one of the most remarkable, warm and moving monuments to Pushkin. It was created for the 100th anniversary of the poet's birth in 1899 by the sculptor Robert Bach.

The monument to Pushkin in the Lyceum garden

The golden gates of the Catherine Palace

The Catherine Palace

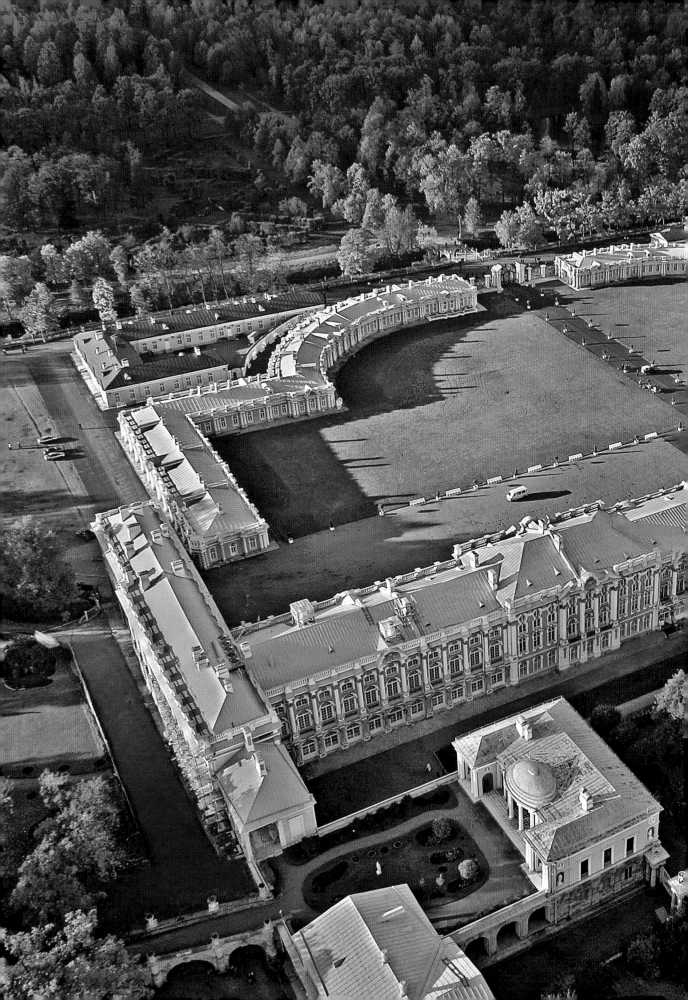

The Cameron Gallery

The Palladian Bridge

The Great Hall
(Bright Gallery) of
the Catherine Palace

The Hermitage
Pavilion

The Amber Room

The Main Staircase

The Krestovsky
Bridge in the
Alexander Park

Pavlovsk

THE Pavlovsk ensemble dates back to the year 1777, when Catherine II presented an estate to her son and heir, Paul (Pavel Petrovich), and his young wife, Maria Feodorovna. In 1779 the renowned architect and dedicated exponent of Neo-Classicism Charles Cameron took on the task of developing the estate. He planned an English landscape park, creating compositional centres in the form of pieces of architecture and in 1782 he embarked on construction of the Pavlovsk palace on the high bank of the Slavianka. He based his design on the immortal ideas of Palladio, adapting the Italian villa type to the harsh northern environment. But Cameron quarrelled with the owners and was unable to finish the project. The interior decoration was entrusted to Vincenzo Brenna. He was also a skilled master, but he lacked the fine Classical taste, that elevated sense of proportion that made Cameron's creation akin to the masterpieces of Antiquity. The word that best describes Brenna's work is "pomp". Mind you, that was what Paul required. After becoming emperor in 1796, he desired to turn the Pavlovsk Palace into a grand residence. Cameron's intimate cosiness gave way to a showy decorativeness, the pompous Empire style, the stern gleam of Roman armour. The spirit of imperial Rome can be sensed everywhere in the palace. Even the Greek Hall was modelled on the villa of the Roman historian Pliny the Younger.

Empress Maria Feodorovna was the true spirit of Pavlovsk. Together with Paul, she planned out every corner of the palace and park. The years passed and the palace and park sparkled in their finished beauty. During strolls in the park the mistress would proudly show guests its most charming spots: the Centaur Bridge across the Slavianka, the Temple of Friendship reflected in the water, its white columns gleaming against a background of trees, the Old Silvia, from which a dozen paths run out in every direction. The open circle is surrounded by statues of the classical muses and gods. They seem to have come out of the dense pine forest and frozen listening to their leader, Apollo, who stands in the middle. After 1812 Maria Feodorovna liked to relax in her Rose Pavilion. There were roses all over – outside the pavilion and in its bright, joyful rooms, where Her Majesty's maids-of-honour flew like nymphs when dancing the waltz.

The Pavlovsk
Palace

The monument
to Paul I

ИМПЕРАТОРУ ПАВЛУ I му
Основателю Павловска

Gatchina

THE name of Gatchina, like Pavlovsk, is inseparable from that of Emperor Paul I, for whom this palace – a gift from his mother, Catherine II, in 1783 – became a refuge. Here he created a special world of his own, orderly, brisk and pleasant, a great contrast to the "debauched" shady world of his mother the Empress, surrounded by her insolent young favourites.

In contrast to Pavlovsk, Gatchino (the original spelling) was not a wild patch of land when Paul received it, but the well-ordered estate of Catherine II's late favourite, Grigory Orlov. The palace had been built by Antonio Rinaldi from 1766. He sensitively detected the character of the place and created a mighty castle faced with grey Pudozh stone on the shore of the large Silver Lake. For chivalrous Paul, who was inclined to be a romantic, the palace was immediately attractive and he called in Brenna who enhanced the "mediaeval" impression by increasing the height of the towers.

The castle's interiors form a striking contrast with the austere exterior. The halls and reception rooms seem full of the architectural music of Neo-Classicism. There is the exquisite White Hall, the gleaming Carrara marble of the Dining-Room, the unusual intricacy and beauty of the parquet in the Throne Room. Gobelins tapestries (a gift from Louis XVI) in the Crimson Drawing-Room are matched in beauty by another of the King's gifts – the light blue Lyonnais silk and the cobalt Sèvres vases that stand in the State Bedchamber.

Located at a distance from the Gatchina Palace is the wonderful Priory Palace, created by Nikolai Lvov as a residence for the prior of the Knights of Malta, whose Grand Master Paul had become.

In 1881, following Alexander II's murder by terrorists, his son, Alexander III, moved here with his family. The Tsar, who acquired the nickname "The Hermit of Gatchina", lived for months at a time in the palace that had been partially reconstructed back in the mid-1800s.

The Gatchina
Palace

The White Hall

Emperor Paul I's
throne

The Priory Palace

Strelna

IN 1717, after Peter I's return from France, work began at Strelna, halfway between Peterhof and St Petersburg, on a project that was no less grand and no less expensive than Peterhof.

Construction had been going on at Strelna for a long time – a wooden wayside palace had been built for Peter on a ridge; labourers under the direction of Italian engineers busied themselves draining the area, laying out a garden and constructing a long jetty. On terraces in front of the wayside palace they made a vegetable plot. This building has miraculously survived down to the present. The park and vegetable garden have been carefully restored. There is a smell of fresh-mown hay; huge pumpkins lie around and a great variety of flowers bloom with careless abandon on the slope of the green hill that is topped by Peter's enchanting little yellow and white palace.

But then in 1717 Peter determined to have a great palace here with "a garden no worse than Versailles" and entrusted the planning first to Carlo Bartolomeo Rastrelli and then to Jean-Baptiste Le Blond. But at some point in the early 1720s Peter suddenly cooled to the idea. The great edifice was reconstructed, suffered two fires, was restored, but never did become a Russian Versailles.

The Konstantinovsky Palace, as it was now known, got a new lease of life in the mid-19th century, when it passed to Grand Duke Konstantin, the son of Emperor Nicholas I. In his time the building acquired the look of a luxurious, showy, if rather eclectic residence and was filled with music. Many outstanding performers played here and after a visit to Strelna r Johann Strauss wrote the Alexandra Waltz in honour of Konstantin's wife and the Terraces of Strelna quadrille.

The last owner of the palace, Konstantin's son, Grand Duke Dmitry, was shot by the Communists in the Peter and Paul Fortress in 1919. For many long years the palace and park presented a spectacle of desolation and were surely destined to perish, had it not been for the decision in 2001 to turn the Konstantinovsky Palace into the state Palace of Congresses complex. In two years the palace was speedily refurbished and given a new lease of life

The Wayside Palace of Peter I

The garden of the Wayside Palace

The Konstantinovsky Palace

The bedroom in the Wayside Palace

The Marble Hall of the Konstantinovsky Palace

Kronstadt

IN THE late autumn of 1703, as soon as the Swedish ships left the mouth of the Neva for the winter, Peter measured the depths in the Gulf of Finland and decided to construct a fort on one of the sandbanks off the island of Kotlin. Early in 1704 he sent a model of the fort from Voronezh, where he was at the time. Originally the fort was constructed of logs and equipped with ships' guns, so that it bore a fair resemblance to a grounded ship. In May 1704 the fort was consecrated and given the name Kronslot (meaning "crown castle" in Dutch). From that moment on the Neva was reliably protected from intruding Swedish ships.

Soon a small strong point was constructed on the western tip of Kotlin, whose garrison together with Kronslot repulsed Swedish attempt to enter the Neva. Then, on 7 October 1723, the fortress of Kronstadt was founded at the eastern end of the island. That day is also considered the birthday of the town of Kronstadt). From that moment, Kronstadt began its evolution into what it is today: the main naval base of Russia's Baltic Fleet.

But the construction of small forts on the sandbanks of the Gulf of Finland also demonstrated its worth and a second – the Citadel or Fort Peter I – was constructed outside the Kronstadt harbour, followed by a third, New Kronslot. In all 21 forts were built, 17 of them surrounded by water. They formed a powerful barrier to any attempt by a hostile fleet to break through to St Petersburg.

Kronstadt itself is a quiet, well-appointed town dominated by the St Nicholas Naval Cathedral constructed in 1913 to a Neo-Byzantine design by Vasily Kosiakov.

That same year a monument was unveiled in front of it to Vice-Admiral Stepan Makarov, who died on the battleship *Petropavlovsk* off Port Arthur in 1904 following a surprise attack by the Japanese navy. The dynamic, even expressive figure was created by Leonid Sherwood. At the Admiral's feet a bronze wave mutates into a symbolic Japanese dragon, dragging the hero into the depths. Nearby, above the Dock Ravine, is the Suspension Bridge constructed in 1900, which visitors to Kronstadt are fond of walking across.

The monument to Peter I in the Petrovsky Park

View of the Petrovsky Harbour from the Winter Landing-Stage

The St Nicholas Naval Cathedral and the monument to Vice-Admiral Makarov

TEXT BY YEVGENY ANISIMOV

ENGLISH TRANSLATION: Paul Williams
EDITOR: T. Lobanova
DESIGN: A. Lobanov
PHOTOGRAPHS: M. Antonova,
S. Bogomiako, N. Goncharova,
V. Davydov, V. Denisov,
A. Lobanov, Ye. Siniaver,
Ye. Mironenko, I. Pushnoi,
I. Litviak, A. Petrosian,
V. Savik, I. Smelov

© Ye. Anisimov, text, 2014
© P. Williams, English translation, 2014
© A. Lobanov, layout and design, 2014
© T. Lobanova, compilation, annotations, 2014
© M. Antonova, S. Bogomiako, N. Goncharova, V. Davydov,
V. Denisov, A. Lobanov, Ye. Siniaver, Ye. Mironenko, I. Pushnoi,
I. Litviak, A. Petrosian, V. Savik, I. Smelov, photographs, 2014
© GOLDEN LION publishing house, 2014

GOLDEN LION PUBLISHING HOUSE
Ulitsa Mira, 3, 197101, St Petersburg, Russia
Tel./Fax: +7 812 493 5207

PRINTED IN RUSSIA